THE Cafe Spice COOKBOOK

84 QUICK AND EASY INDIAN RECIPES FOR EVERYDAY MEALS

HARI NAYAK

photography by
JACK TURKEL

TUTTLE Publishing

Tokyo | Rutland, Vermont | Singapore

CONTENTS

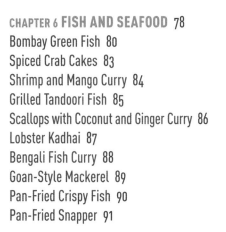

THE CAFÉ SPICE STORY

Far from the land of its birth and the influences that shaped it, Indian food is now a five billion dollar industry in the West and growing rapidly. Westerners' exposure to Indian cuisine has come a long way since the early days of inexpensive curry houses. Since then, more professional Indians have settled overseas, and non-Indians have had the opportunity to travel to India and discover the authentic and diverse flavors of local foods.

Restaurants have become more upscale, and it is common now to find places specializing in regional cooking from, for example, Kerala or Chennai or Bombay. At the same time, Indian chefs with formal culinary training are developing their own styles of preparation using locally-available products and European-inspired methods. The new generation of Indian chef might even consciously avoid commonly known dishes such as Chicken Tikka Masala, Korma, Vindaloo, and Madras Curry, despite the fact that a huge number of diners still seek out those traditional restaurant dishes. I actually tried Tikka Masala and Madras Curry for the first time when I came to New York from India and had my first meal on "Curry Hill" on Lexington Ave. between 27th and 28th St.— and it was an experience, to say the least! I had never eaten anything like that in India, and yet these are the most popular and best-known Indian dishes in America.

As a student at the Culinary Institute of America (CIA) in New York, I dreamed of changing the way Americans view Indian cuisine. Most Americans are intimidated, some are curious, and some are addicted to curry. But almost all non-Indians I meet are eager to explore further and learn more about our cuisine. Indian cuisine retains its exotic image today, and yet many people only know what they get in restaurants. I was eager to take up the challenge and be an ambassador who could make this cuisine more accessible to the average person. By simplifying a few processes and adding new creative twists to the classic recipes, I began publishing books with easy recipes that allow a home cook with a normal Western kitchen to recreate classic Indian dishes with all the flavor but none of the fear or fuss.

After graduating from the CIA and while working with different international food service companies, I began to envision a new business opportunity—to develop a new Indian food brand created specifically for the American market. The interest in Indian cuisine was rapidly growing globally, and I could anticipate the natural progression towards demand for a range of food products that are Indian in flavor and design.

This is how I met the founder of Café Spice, Sushil Malhotra. I remember vividly my first meeting with him at the Café Spice bistro near New York University (NYU) in New York City. An elderly man, but with the passion and drive of a young entrepreneur, his energy impressed me. He reminded me of my father. At the threshold of a career in the food industry, I envisioned Indian food could eventually becoming mainstream and as popular as other ethnic cuisines such as Italian, Chinese, or Mexican. Here was a man who had exactly the same vision, many years before I was born! It amazed me how forward-thinking he was. That meeting is the main reason I am sitting down to write this book today. Not only are Malhotras my extended family in this country, but Sushil's affection, warmth, and trust have been a key inspiration in my career.

Sushil and his wife Lata live in Westchester, NY. They have two daughters and a son. Sushil fondly calls me "Beta" (son in Hindi), and that makes me feel very special. I work closely with Lata, who helps me create new recipes for Café Spice, along with their son Sameer Malhotra,

who runs the operation. We work as friends with the shared goal of contributing to the success of the enterprise. This common purpose makes us all work that much harder, and we make a great team.

Sushil's story is a classic entrepreneur's tale of passion, knowledge, and determination to overcome every hurdle and challenge to reach a desired goal. He is at the top of America's Indian food business now, but his journey wasn't easy. He left India during the 1960s in an era of droughts, oil crisis, refugees, and a collapsing currency. Sushil managed to get a scholarship to study at City College in New York City, where he arrived in 1966, just 17 years old. He earned a degree in engineering and went to work for Shell and Disney, later earning an MBA from NYU's Stern School of Business.

Conditions in India during the following decade did not show any signs of improvement. Many of his family members also migrated to the Big Apple and together with his father, Sushil opened a small spice business that supplied South Asian spices and chutneys to New York's curry houses. The father-son duo opened a shop on Lexington Avenue and stored their spices in their Jackson Heights, Queens garage. Sushil used his weekends helping his father deliver chutney and spices to Indian restaurants in Manhattan and Queens.

In 1976, Sushil ditched engineering to become a full-time restaurateur. Indian cuisine in America had not yet changed much in the 70s. Sushil saw an opportunity, brought in a couple of investment partners, and opened his first Indian restaurant on Park Avenue. It was called Akbar and as a fine dining establishment was meant to represent India in its glory. Diners initially didn't take well to the concept; they found its doorman and the huge, black doors intimidating. But after a glorious review in the *New York Times* by food critic Craig Claiborne, customers poured through the black doors, and there was no looking back.

Nine years after opening Akbar, Sushil felt that it had "peaked." He sold it and opened a new place called Dawat, with Madhur Jaffrey as chef and consultant. At the time, Jaffrey was called the "Julia Child of Indian food." This second effort was an even bigger hit than Akbar. Its celebrity guest lists included Michael Jackson, Derek Jeter, Donald Trump, and Whitney Houston. I have heard many heart-warming stories from Jaffrey over dinner at the Malhotra residence, where she was a frequent guest. In fact, a recipe for Durupadi Jagtianiin in several of Madhur Jaffrey's cookbooks is fondly named the "Nani mom" recipe, after Lata's mother .

Later in the '90s, Sushil got out of fine dining and began opening casual bistros. The first Café Spice opened its doors in Manhattan in 1995. Others soon followed in Philadelphia, Jersey City, and Gaithersburg, Maryland. The business model was to open close to college campuses, especially those with large foreign student populations. Although these establishments were very successful, the team closed them in 2010 to concentrate on quick-service restaurants and on supplying supermarkets and other retail outlets. Today, Café Spice is a successful 30-million-dollar enterprise that is growing 20 percent a year in the booming Indian food market.

More than just another restaurant cookbook, this book is about the family that has made Café Spice such a successful brand. It is about celebrating the success of a company that celebrates Indian food, and about the enterprising ideas that have enabled Café Spice to be such a pioneering brand in the food business. It is also about the passion of a family whose mission is to "give Indian cooking to the world" in a real and authentic way. The passion of the Café Spice owners has inspired me to write this cookbook.

The handpicked recipes in this book are all simple to make and contain some of my own creative twists and substitutions that make them easier for the home cook to prepare. I have included several of my own signature dishes, but most of the creations are from the Café Spice repertoire using its signature spice blends. For those of you who are familiar with Café Spice products and my own brand of chutneys and spice rubs, this book will give you the opportunity to learn how these products are used to make food that is tasty and also beautiful! The book also contains many recipes inspired by my family and friends. I hope that all of you enjoy cooking from this book as much as I have enjoyed creating it.

—Hari Nayak

A Few Simple Techniques

The heart and soul of Indian cooking is mastering the unique and imaginative use of spices, seasonings, and flavorings and learning the nitty-gritty of Indian cooking techniques. You will already be familiar with many of those techniques from your own everyday cooking. The main ones are steaming (*dum*), tempering (*tarhka*), roasting (*bhunnana*), frying (*talna*), and sautéing (*bhunao*). Other common techniques are roasting and grinding spices; browning onions, garlic, and meats; and handling sauces. Each of these methods, or a combination of two or three or even all, may be necessary to prepare an Indian dish. They are not hard to master, but it's important to understand the basic principles of each.

BROWNING Most Indian recipes require browning onions by frying them over medium-high heat. Evenly browned onions are more flavorful and give sauces the desired rich, deep reddish-brown color. The same goes for garlic—the flavor of garlic is quite amazing if it is fried in oil until it turns golden brown. For the best flavor and color, meat is also browned. Browning also sears the meat, which makes it juicy. I like to brown marinated meat before combining it with other ingredients. If I am cooking a larger quantity, I brown a few pieces of meat at a time in hot oil and set them aside. I then add the browned meat and all the cooking juices back into the pan with the other ingredients and let it finish cooking in the sauce.

DEEP-FRYING (*TALNA*) *Talna* refers to deep-frying, Indian style. Generally, Indian cooks use a *kadhai*—a deep pan with a rounded bottom similar to a wok. Unlike a deep-fat fryer, the size and shape of the kadhai does not allow large quantities of food to be fried at one time. The result is even frying. When deep-frying, oil should be heated to between 325° and 350°F (160° and 180°C). This temperature is crucial—if the oil is too hot, the outside of food will brown very quickly, leaving the insides uncooked; and if the oil is not hot enough, the foods will absorb the oil and become greasy. When frying, do not crowd the pan; fry the food in batches if necessary. Use a slotted spatula or spoon when removing fried food from the oil and hold each piece against the edge of the pan for a few seconds to allow excess oil to drain back into the pan. Place fried foods on a tray lined with paper towels to drain. If you intend to reuse the oil, turn off the heat as soon as you're finished frying and let the oil cool completely. Using a fine-mesh strainer, strain the oil into an airtight container. Store the oil at room temperature.

ROASTING (*BHUNNANA*) Traditionally in Indian cooking, roasting is done in a charcoal-fired *tandoor* (clay oven), which gives a unique flavor to roasted meats, breads, and vegetables. The juices of the meats drip onto the charcoal which sizzles and creates smoke that gives the food its unique flavor. For home cooking, an open charcoal grill is good substitute when cooking meat kebabs, vegetables, and

Roasting spices

paneer (cheese), though the flavor is milder than that achieved in a tandoor. An oven can be used to make breads and to roast marinated meats and vegetables. A good example that showcases the roasting technique is Tandoori Spiced Roasted Chicken (page 98).

ROASTING AND GRINDING OF SPICES
Roasting is the key to bringing out the flavor of spices. Roasting spices removes the raw smell typical of untreated spices and intensifies their flavors by heating up essential oils. All you need is a small, heavy-bottomed skillet (cast iron works great). No oil is used when roasting spices. Whole spices are put in a dry skillet and roasted over medium heat until they turn a shade or two darker and become aromatic. The spices are then immediately removed from the hot skillet to avoid over-roasting. In my kitchen, I generally buy spices whole and then grind them myself as needed. Because spices retain their flavor and aroma much longer when left whole than when ground, grinding roasted spices in small batches is the ideal way to use them and imparts the greatest possible flavor to dishes. Traditionally in Indian kitchens, spices are ground on heavy grinding stones or with a mortar and pestle. To save time, I use a spice grinder, though a coffee grinder works equally well.

SAUTÉING (*BHUNAO*)
Unlike classic French sautéing, Indian sautéing, or *bhunao*, is a combination of sautéing, stir-frying, and light stewing. It is the process of cooking over medium to high heat, adding small quantities of liquid, such as water or tomato purée, and stirring constantly to prevent the ingredients from sticking. Almost every Indian recipe needs bhunao at some stage, and some at more than one stage. Generally, ingredients like onions, ginger, garlic, tomatoes, and spices require bhunao. The purpose of this technique is to extract the flavor of each of the ingredients in combination with spices, as well as to ensure that the *masala* (spice mix) is fully cooked before adding the main ingredient.

Sometimes a main ingredient such as poultry, meats, or vegetables may also require bhunao. The process of making masala is complete only when the fat leaves the masala—very critical step in Indian cooking. Traditionally a kadhai is used for this technique. I find that a heavy-bottomed saucepan or another deep-sided pan, such as a braiser or Dutch oven, works just as well. Recipes such as Curried Chicken Meatball (page 100), Easy Lamb Curry (page 101) and Chicken Tikka Masala (page 97) are good examples of this technique.

STEAMING (*DUM*)
Dum cooking has been described as the "maturing of a dish." In this technique, food is very slowly cooked in its own steam. Traditionally, the lid was sealed to the cooking vessel with a flour-and-water paste to make sure moisture was trapped within. The vessel was slightly buried in hot coals and, to ensure the food was evenly surrounded by heat, some hot coals were placed on the lid. Today, the modern oven provides even heat. The dish is first cooked on a stove top and then well-sealed and placed in the oven to continue to cook in its own steam. The advantage of dum cooking is that since the vapors cannot escape, the food retains all its delicate flavor and aroma. One of the most common and popular dishes prepared using this technique is the famous rice dish, called *biriyani*.

TEMPERING (*TARHKA*)
This technique is unique to Indian cooking. Oil is heated until very hot and a mixture of whole spices with or without chopped garlic and ginger is added. Hot oil has an extraordinary ability to extract and retain the essence, aroma, and the flavor of spices and herbs. This process is performed either at the beginning of cooking or after the dish is finished. If done after a dish is cooked, the prepared tempering is poured sizzling hot over the dish to add a burst of flavor (this technique is sometimes done when preparing dals). The seasonings that are most commonly used for tempering include cumin seeds, black mustard seeds, fennel seeds, dried red chilies, cloves, cinnamon, cardamom, and bay leaves as well as chopped up ginger, garlic, and fresh or dried curry leaves. The ingredients are usually added in rapid succession, rarely together. The purpose of adding tempering ingredients sequentially is to ensure that each ingredient is fully cooked, and thus its flavor fully extracted into the oil before the next ingredient is added. This method also allows for longer-cooking ingredients or spices to be added first, and shorter-cooking ingredients or spices last, to prevent their burning. The crackling of the spices or a change in their color indicates that the process is complete, unless fresh herbs and vegetables are also being used. A few of the many recipes in this book that use this technique of tempering are South Indian Cabbage Slaw (page 33), Green Pea Relish (page 30), South Indian Lentils and Vegetables (page 56), Coconut Rice (page 112) and Lemon Rice with Peanuts (page 114).

Some Helpful Tools and Tips

You do not need special kitchen tools or cookware to cook authentic Indian food at home. All you need is a well-equipped kitchen with sturdy skillets, pots and pans with lids, tongs, good knives, graters, mixing bowls, a rolling pin, a perforated spoon, a sieve, a strainer, and a citrus squeezer. I like to use an Indian spice box to hold my most frequently used spices and spice blends: Café Spice Garam Masala (page 22), cumin seeds, mustard seeds, Asian red chili powder, or cayenne pepper, and turmeric. The box sits on my kitchen counter where I can quickly grab a pinch of spice when needed. I generally use nonstick pots, saucepans, and skillets when cooking Indian food at home because of the relatively long cooking time. Some ingredients, such as spices, onions, ginger, garlic, and tomatoes—which are typically cooked in small quantities of liquid or fat—tend to stick to conventional pans. To prevent sticking if you have regular pots and pans, make sure they are heavy-bottomed and sturdy, stir the food frequently, and add more cooking oil as needed. The following additional tools are not crucial, but they will make cooking Indian food a lot simpler and quicker.

BLENDER When it comes to combining liquids with fresh herbs or spices for sauces, pastes, or purées, there is nothing more effective than a blender. Unlike a blender with a broad base that is ideal for blended drinks, one with a narrow, tapered base (or basically straight sides) works well to purée thick sauces and pastes. I also use it to grind large amount of whole spices. I discovered how surprisingly well a blender works when I made large quantities of my Café Spice Garam Masala (page 22) to give as gifts for family and friends. I prefer a glass blender, because plastic absorbs aromas from the spices and herbs. I also have a hand-held blender, also known as an immersion blender or "smart stick," that I use to purée vegetables, lentils, or beans. It is ideal for preparing puréed soups or dals, such as Green Pea Soup (page 50) or Cauliflower and Curry Soup (page 54), becasue you can purée the food directly in the pan. You need not wait for the liquid to cool, which is advisable when transferring hot liquid to a blender, and it saves you the task of cleaning up a messy blender.

Rolling pin

Grater

Perforated spoon

ELECTRIC FOOD PROCESSOR The traditional grinding stone of Indian kitchens, which is heavy and labor intensive, is now replaced with the modern food processor—a time-saving tool par excellence for busy cooks. Essential ingredients like onion, chili peppers, garlic, and ginger can be made into pastes very quickly in these electrically powered machines. The food processor can be used to chop or mince vegetables and fresh herbs, cutting down considerably on prep time. I recommend a food processor that has a capacity of 7 to 10 cups. To pulverize small quantities of ingredients, make sure the blades sit close to the bottom. However, when chopping very small amounts of fresh garlic, onions, chili peppers, or ginger, a chef's knife is more practical.

ELECTRIC SPICE GRINDER OR COFFEE GRINDER I highly recommend investing in a spice or coffee grinder. It is one of the most important tools that you will use in Indian cooking. I use it to coarsely or finely grind dry whole spices. It works in seconds, and cleanup —not always necessary after each spice—is very simple. I personally use the Cuisinart Spice and Nut Grinder, which is available for under $40. The ability of electric coffee grinders to grind coffee beans also makes them ideally suited for a wide range of spices, such as cumin seeds, cinnamon sticks (broken up), cardamom, and bay leaves. They can grind as little as a teaspoon to as much as half a cup. For larger volumes of whole spices, a blender works surprisingly well. I strongly recommend that you invest in a spice grinder or coffee grinder as it will make your cooking process very simple and the results very flavorful. If do you use a coffee grinder, reserve it for spices only; otherwise, you will end up with cumin-flavored coffee.

CAST-IRON SKILLETS AND GRIDDLES Small cast-iron skillets are ideal for dry roasting spices because they brown them evenly without the need to add any cooking fat or liquid. Always preheat your cast-iron pan before frying in it. A large cast-iron skillet or griddle is excellent for making Indian flatbreads such as Whole Wheat Griddle Bread (page 122). Traditionally, these breads are cooked in a *tava*, a round, concave, cast-iron griddle that is available in South Asian grocery stores. New cast-iron pans should be seasoned before use. To season a cast-iron pan, rub a relatively thin coat of neutral oil all around the inside of the pan. Place the cast-iron pan upside-down in a cold oven with a sheet of aluminum foil on the bottom to catch any drips. Set the oven to 300°– 400°F (150º–200ºC) and let the pan heat for 30–60 minutes. Once done, let the pan cool to room temperature. Repeating this process several times is recommended. Never put cold liquid into a very hot cast-iron pan; doing so might crack and damage the pan. Cast iron is a great alternative to nonstick cooking surfaces. Cast iron can be pre-heated to temperatures that will brown meat and will withstand oven temperatures well above what is considered safe for nonstick pans. You can cook almost any food in cast-iron cookware. It is a natural nonstick surface, and if your pan is seasoned correctly, food will not stick to it.

KADHAI, KARAHI OR KADAI
This is a deep pan similar in shape to the Chinese wok. A kadhai is traditionally made out of cast iron although other materials such as stainless steel and copper are sometimes used, and nonstick versions also exist. It is ideal for deep-frying, Indian style (talna), because the rounded bottom allows you to use a relatively small quantity of oil while providing enough depth in the center to submerge foods. The kadhai is also used for stir-frying vegetables. There are decorative ones that are best used for serving, not cooking. A small wok about 12 inches (30 cm) in diameter is a close substitute for a kadhai.

An Introduction to Indian Ingredients

The following is a description of some of the most commonly used Indian ingredients. Many of the ingredients and spices used in this book are found in well-stocked supermarkets. These include cumin, coriander, turmeric, mace, black pepper, ginger, paprika, cayenne pepper, cloves, cinnamon, and cardamom. Some others are carried in South Asian or Indian food markets or are available by mail and on the internet (see Shopping Guide, page 140).

Indian cuisine has always been very receptive to spices and ingredients from other cuisines and cultures. For example, in India and in Indian homes around the world, it is very common to use Sriracha chili sauce or soy sauce to jazz up Indian stir-fry dishes or dipping sauces that are inspired by other Asian cuisines. (See Spiced Crab Cakes, page 82, and Dried Bombay Beef, page 106.)

In this book I use some ingredients that are not used in a traditional Indian kitchen. Olive oil is one of them. Even though in most cases Indian recipes call for any neutral-flavored vegetable oil (for example, canola, safflower, or corn oil), olive oil is a healthier alternative. I use it often to drizzle over salads (Sweet Potato and Sprout Salad, page 44) and sometimes for lighter cooking and simple vegetable dishes.

Traditionally whole-milk yogurt is hung in a muslin cloth to drain out all the whey to create the creamy, thick yogurt known as "hung curd" that is ideal for many authentic Indian recipes—particularly to marinate chicken or meats and make creamy sauces and dips. Rather than take the time to hang plain yogurt at home, I use either sour cream or the increasingly available thick, Greek-style plain yogurt. Both are perfect alternatives for the Indian thick, creamy yogurt.

Storage Tips for Spices and Herbs

Ideally, it is best to buy all dry spices in their whole form. Whole spices will stay fresh generally five to six months longer than pre-ground spices. It's a good habit to smell ground spices before using them; if their smell is very faint, it's time to replace them or grind a fresh batch. Both whole and ground spices should be stored in a cool, dry, dark place in tightly covered jars. Freshly ground spices are not the same as pre-ground, store-bought spices. Freshly ground spices are far superior in flavor and aroma to pre-ground spices. Another difference is volume: Freshly ground spices have less density tablespoon for tablespoon and less volume ounce for ounce than pre-ground spices, which settle over time. You might think you would need to use more of the freshly ground spice to compensate for the greater weight of the settled, and therefore denser, pre-ground bottled spice. But because pre-ground spices are so much less potent than freshly ground, the difference in volume is not of consequence. If anything, you might need to add more of the pre-ground spice.

To prolong the life span of fresh herbs, such as fresh coriander (cilantro) and mint, wash the leaves and dry with a paper towel until the leaves are mostly, but not completely, dry. Store refrigerated, wrapped in a paper towel, inside a zip-lock bag.

Asafetida The dried, gum-like resin from the rhizome of a giant fennel-like plant is sold in both lump and ground forms. It is used in very small quantities because of its strong and pungent flavor, which is somewhat like garlic. I use and recommend the ground version because it comes mixed with rice flour and turmeric powder to mellow the flavor.

Asian Red Chili Powder or **Cayenne Pepper** This is a red powder made from grinding the dried, red skins of several types of chili peppers. In India, it is simply called "chili powder." You can substitute cayenne pepper, which is commonly available in supermarkets. The Indian chili powder, which is darker in color than cayenne pepper, is available in Indian grocery stores. It adds a spicy flavor to dishes.

Bay Leaves These are long, oval, pointed and smooth leaves of a hardy evergreen shrub. The leaves are dark green when fresh and turn olive green when dry. The fresh leaves are very mild and do not develop their full flavor until several weeks after being picked and dried. They are often used whole or sometimes ground in curries and rice dishes. They are an important ingredient in the Indian spice blend, garam masala. Bay leaves are also a common fixture in the cooking of many European cuisines (particularly those of the Mediterranean), as well as North and South American cuisines. The bay leaf that is commonly available in North America is similar in appearance to the Indian bay leaf, but its flavor and fragrance are milder than the Indian one. If you cannot find Indian bay leaves, which are often found only in Indian grocery stores, you may substitute regular bay leaves. The difference is very subtle and will not be apparent in the final result.

Cardamom The cardamom plant is native to India and Sri Lanka and is also cultivated in Guatemala, Mexico, Indonesia, and other areas of southern Asia. Cardamom pods are harvested just before they are ripe and are allowed to dry in the sun or sometimes in drying machines. There are two distinct types of cardamom pods used in Indian cooking—the small, green pod and large, black pod. The green pods are the most common and have an exceptional flavor. I use the green pods in all the recipes in this book. Black cardamom pods are used in Indian rice and meat dishes, but they are not as commonly available. Cardamom pods are used in almost every part of the cuisine, from savory dishes to curries and desserts. When using cardamom for desserts, the seeds are extracted from the pods and ground to a powder. For curries, stews, or rice dishes, the whole pod can be added directly to the food. The sharp and bitter taste of cardamom mellows to a warming, sweet taste as it cooks. In the West, ground cardamom is more readily available than the pods, whereas in India, it is more typical to find whole pods. The quality of pre-ground cardamom is not as good as from seeds freshly ground at home. Once the pods are opened or the seeds ground, the flavor and aroma of the cardamom are lost very quickly. I especially recommend freshly grinding the seeds for the dessert and beverage recipes, where the spice often plays a key role.

Chili Peppers, Fresh, Green There are more than 150 varieties of chili peppers in the world. That's a lot to keep track of, but as a general rule, the smaller ones are hotter than the larger ones. The two most common chilies used in Indian cooking are the cayenne and Thai. Cayenne pepper is green when fresh and red when dried. The Thai variety, sometimes known as "bird's eye," is smaller and hotter. The serrano chili is more widely available in the United States and is a good alternative to the cayenne and Thai, though it is milder. If you cannot find fresh cayenne, Thai, or serrano chili peppers, simply use what's available. Fresh chilies are one of the most important ingredients for providing pungency in Indian cuisine. In many regions in India, fresh, green chilies are served raw with the food. Often I like to reduce the heat by removing the inner membrane and seeds and use only the skin. Chopping a fresh chili releases capsaicin, and the finer you chop it, the hotter the taste. Sometimes I slit the chilies open, but leave the seeds intact to release a gentler heat.

Chili Peppers, Dried, Red These are whole, dried red hot chilies, about 1 1/2–2 in (4–5 cm) long that are usually added to hot oil to infuse it with their strong flavor. A quick contact with hot oil enhances and intensifies the flavor of the skins. Most chilies start off green and turn red as they age. The Indian dried red chilies are similar to most common types such as the cayenne and chile de arbol.

Cinnamon This highly fragrant spice is the dried inner bark of the laurel tree. An important ingredient in Indian cooking, it imparts a pleasant aroma to foods. It is sold in powder and stick forms. The whole sticks are used to flavor meats, curry dishes, and rice dishes as well as teas.

Cloves These are the dried, unopened buds of a tropical tree. Deep reddish-brown cloves add a strong fragrance to rice and grain recipes and are an important ingredient in garam masala. They are lightly fried in hot oil, which perfumes the food cooked in it.

Coconut Milk, Coconut Meat,

Shredded Coconut In my recipes I use coconut milk, coconut meat, and shredded coconut. Coconut milk is produced by crushing the thick, white coconut meat and mixing it with water. The result is then drained, and the soaked coconut meat squeezed to extract the liquid. As the milk sits, the fat rises to the surface. This fat is skimmed off and sold separately as coconut cream. The cream is much richer and thicker than the milk. Coconut milk and coconut cream are both sold in cans. When using coconut milk for savory recipes, make sure it is not sweetened. Sweetened milk or cream is used in making pastries and cocktails. I prefer to use full-fat coconut milk rather than the "lite" version that is not as flavorful or creamy. Before opening a can of coconut milk, make sure to shake it well as the cream will have risen to the top; shaking the can incorporates the cream into the thinner milk-like liquid to create a smooth, even consistency. Once the can is opened make sure you store it in the refrigerator, covered, and use it within 2–3 days since it spoils quickly.

Packaged, shredded coconut (sometimes labeled "grated") is available frozen, which is the next best option to freshly grated and dried or "desiccated." For the recipes in this book, be sure to purchase unsweetened shredded coconut. While dried unsweetened coconut is easy to find in most supermarkets or health food stores, frozen shredded coconut is available only in Southeast Asian or Indian grocery stores. The dried shredded coconut, however, has significantly less flavor than the frozen or fresh forms and does not give the creamy texture that is desired in Indian curries and stews. If you only have access to dried unsweetened shredded coconut, soak ½ cup (50 g) of the dried coconut in ½ cup (125 ml) of boiling water for about 15 minutes. Drain the excess water before use. Note that ½ cup of dried coconut is comparable to 1 cup of freshly shredded or frozen shredded coconut.

Freshly shredded or grated coconut will provide the best flavor and texture in Indian dishes. This requires purchasing a coconut and cracking it apart at home. Here is how to grate fresh coconut at home: Start with a clean looking coconut without cracks or any overpowering or rancid smell. It should feel heavy and full of water. You can shake the coconut to hear the water swish. Place the coconut on a clean, heavy wooden cutting board or a clean concrete block. Holding the coconut in one hand, tap the coconut lightly on all sides with a hammer to dislodge the insides from the hard brown shell. Then carefully but forcefully hit the shell with the hammer to break it open. Now most of the hard shell should separate from the coconut. Carefully pry off the meat from the brown outer shell with the tip of a well-rounded, blunt knife. Grate the coconut meat using a handheld grater.

Coriander Leaves, Fresh Also known as cilantro, this annual in the parsley family is one of the most commonly used herbs in Indian cuisine. It is generally used uncooked for garnishes, marinades, and chutneys. Many dishes also incorporate fresh coriander leaves at various stages of cooking, a process that softens the sharp flavor and aroma of the herb. Fresh coriander leaves are highly perishable and prone to wilting. See "Storage Tips for Spices and Herbs," page 12.

Coriander Seeds are ribbed peppercorn-sized and -shaped, pale green to light brown–colored seeds of the coriander (cilantro) plant. They are extremely aromatic, with a spicy hint. Their taste and aroma, however, are in no way similar to the leaves of the coriander plant. I always keep them in small quantities in airtight containers, as they lose their flavor with exposure and age. Coriander seeds are also available in a ground form.

Cucumbers Used widely in Indian kitchens, cucumbers can be served with any Indian meal. They can always be found in my refrigerator and are a summertime favorite. The cooling, clean flavor matches well with foods like chilies, cilantro, cream, garlic, lemon, lime, mint, olive oil, onions, sour cream, tomatoes, vinegar, and yogurt. I like to cut them into little finger-sized wedges and serve with a sprinkle of salt, black pepper, Asian red chili powder or cayenne pepper, and a heavy dose of fresh squeezed lemon juice.

When purchasing cucumbers, look for a smooth, brightly colored skin. Cucumbers keep well in a plastic bag in the refrigerator for up to ten days. I prefer to use the long, seedless variety called "English cucumbers," and though called seedless, they actually have very small seeds. They are usually sold shrink-wrapped. Unlike the common garden-variety salad cucumber, these cucumbers can be eaten without peeling or seeding.

Cumin Seeds These seeds are the

best-known and most widely used spice in Indian cuisine. They are either fried whole in hot oil or dry roasted and then used whole or finely ground, depending on the recipe. Cumin is warm and intense and has an almost nutty aroma.

Curry Leaves Curry leaves originate from the kari tree, a sub-tropical tree native to India. They are used similarly to bay leaves—mainly as an aromatic and flavoring for most curries and soups. They are widely used in dishes along the southern coastal regions of India. When starting a curry or soup dish, curry leaves are placed in hot oil and fried until crisp, which makes the oil and the leaves intensely flavorful. In India, it is more common to use fresh curry leaves rather than dried ones. You can purchase fresh curry leaves in Indian grocery stores. Dried curry leaves can be purchased from specialty gourmet stores or online (see Shopping Guide, page 140). I recommend always buying fresh instead of dried leaves. The best way to store fresh curry leaves is to wash them and pat them mostly dry with a paper towel. Store refrigerated, wrapped in a paper towel inside a zip-lock bag. They will stay fresh for up to a month. For extended use, air dry them completely and store in an airtight container.

Split Red Lentils (Masoor Dal)

Split Pigeon Peas (Toor Dal)

Mung Bean (Mung Dal)

Split Yellow Peas (Chana Dal)

Dried Legumes (Lentils, Dried Beans, and Peas) In India, all types of dried legumes—be they lentils, peas or beans—are known as *dals*. They are an integral part of Indian meals, being economical; highly nutritious; very low in fat; and a good source of carbohydrates, proteins, fibers, minerals, and vitamins. Dals are a good substitute for meat, which has more fat and cholesterol. Many common varieties of dals, such as chickpeas (*kabuli chana*), kidney beans (*rajmah*), whole green lentils (*sabut moong*), and cow peas (black-eyed peas) are available in conventional supermarkets. Some not-so-common varieties used in Indian cooking include pigeon peas (*toor dal*), split black gram, aka "black lentils" (*urad dal*), split green lentils (*moong dal*), split red lentils (*masoor dal*), and split yellow peas (*chana dal*). For these, a trip to an Indian grocery

store or an online purchase is necessary (see Shopping Guide, page 140).

Dal dishes come in various forms—thin and soupy (South Indian Lentils and Vegetables, page 56), thick and creamy (Homestyle Dal with Pumpkin, page 60), and hearty and comforting (Chickpea Curry with Sweet Potato, page 54)—and may be the basis of a salad (Chickpea, Mango and Watercress Salad, page 45).

There is nothing more comforting and soulful than a bowl of dal topped with some steamed rice. I incorporate dals into my everyday meals—both Indian and non-Indian. I cook my dried legumes the old fashioned way in my kitchen, using a pressure cooker. Though this technique is not so popular in North American and Europe, I urge you to give pressure cooking a try: It uses less liquid, has faster cooking times, and the food retains

more vitamins and minerals. I can assure you that once you get used to a pressure cooker, you will be eating more dals as part of your daily meals, especially the longer-cooking types. Anticipating that not everyone will have a pressure cooker or be inclined to use one, the recipes in this book call for common kitchenware, such as saucepans or pots. If you want to experiment with a pressure cooker, simply follow the instructions provided with it; you will find that cooking time is reduced by more than 50 percent!

I often stock my pantry with canned legumes, which I find to be an acceptable substitute for dried, and very convenient when I'm in a rush. For the dal recipes in this book, I include the option of using commonly available canned peas or beans. Make sure to drain and rinse them thoroughly before using them.

Fennel Seeds These are the oval, pale greenish-yellow seeds of the common fennel plant, a member of parsley family. They are sweetly aromatic and have an anise-like flavor. In Indian cooking, they are used whole and ground in both sweet and savory dishes. Roasted fennel seeds are sometimes sugarcoated and chewed as a digestive and mouth freshener after Indian meals. They are readily available in most grocery stores.

Fenugreek Leaves Known as *methi* when fresh and *kasoori methi* when dried, these leaves are extensively used in Indian cuisine. The slightly perfumed and bitter flavor of the leaves goes very well with curries. The leaves are sold fresh when in season or dried in packets year round in Indian markets. The dried leaves can also be purchased online (see Shopping Guide, page 140). Frozen chopped fenugreek greens are also now available at some Indian grocery stores. I use the dried version—kasoori methi— in the recipes in this book because of its unique flavor and strong taste. In comparison, fresh methi (young leaves and sprouts of fenugreek) has a very mild flavor. When fresh, the leaves are eaten as greens and are commonly cooked with potatoes, spinach, and paneer and eaten with *roti* or *naan*

(breads). The dried leaves have a bitter taste and strong aroma and are used in small amounts to flavor dishes. There is no real substitute for this ingredient in Indian recipes, and so I have made its use optional throughout the book.

Fenugreek Seeds The fenugreek seeds are bitter, yellowish-brown, tiny seeds that provide commercial curry powders their distinctive aroma. They are used in small quantities because of their strong flavor. In the southern part of India, the seeds are often oil-roasted and then ground to create a bitter balance in curries; in eastern India, the seeds are stir-fried whole. They are available only in Southeast Asian or Indian grocery stores.

Garlic A close relative to onions, shallots, and leeks, garlic has been used throughout recorded history for both culinary and medicinal purposes. It has a characteristic pungent, spicy flavor that mellows and sweetens

considerably with cooking. Garlic powder is not a substitute for fresh garlic in traditional Indian cooking. Whole bulbs of garlic will keep for several months or more when stored at room temperature in a dry, dark place that has ample air circulation. Keep in mind, however, that garlic's shelf life decreases once you start removing cloves from the bulb. Storing garlic uncovered, such as in a wire-mesh basket inside your cupboard is ideal. You can also store garlic in a paper or mesh bag. Just be sure there is plenty of dry air and little light to inhibit sprouting. To avoid mold, do not refrigerate or store garlic in plastic bags.

Ginger A knobby, pale-brown rhizome of a perennial tropical plant, ginger is available fresh, dried, ground into a powder and as a preserved stem. Ground ginger or preserved ginger is almost never used in Indian cooking. Fresh ginger root has no aroma, but once you peel or cut it, it emits a warm, woody aroma with citrus undertones. When used fresh, it has a peppery hot bite to it. Fresh ginger is used throughout India and is a very common ingredient in Indian cooking. It is often ground into a paste, finely chopped, or made into juice. We use chopped

ginger to stir-fry vegetables, crushed ginger or ginger paste in meat stews and legumes, and thinly sliced slivers of raw ginger to sprinkle over curries just before serving. While shopping for fresh ginger, look for a hard and heavy root that snaps easily into pieces. Avoid dry, shriveled roots that feel light for their size. Keep fresh ginger in the refrigerator crisper in a plastic bag with a paper towel to absorb moisture (to prevent mold, change the towel occasionally). The root will last for two or three weeks. To extend its life, you can freeze ginger. You don't even need to defrost it, and ginger is much easier to grate when frozen.

Ghee This is the Indian version of clarified butter—that is, butter from which milk solids are removed. Ghee is one of the primary cooking fats used in India. Unlike regular clarified butter, the process of making ghee involves melting the butter over a low heat and then simmering it until all the moisture has evaporated, and the milk solids have separated from the fat. The milk solids are then removed, leaving a pure fat that is excellent for deep-frying because of its high smoke point. I just love the way ghee infuses food with a delicious flavor and aroma. It has a buttery and a nutty flavor. I often add a few drops to hot rice dishes, dals, and curries as finishing oil. Ghee has a very long shelf life and at room temperature will keep for 4–6 months. Store it in a clean, airtight plastic or glass jar. Ghee is commonly available in Indian grocery stores and is typically sold in glass or plastic jars as a solid, butter-like fat. In many recipes in this book, I have called for ghee, which I feel brings out the best flavor of those dishes. If you do not have ghee, substitute a mixture of equal parts of unsalted butter and neutral-flavored oil.

To Make Ghee at Home: Melt 1 lb (450 g) of unsalted butter in a heavy-bottomed, medium-size saucepan over medium-low heat. Simmer, stirring occasionally, until the milk solids turn a rich golden color and settle to the bottom of the pan, about 15–20 minutes. Initially, the butter will foam and as it simmers the foam will subside. Pass the mixture through a fine-mesh strainer lined with cheesecloth or muslin into a sterilized jar. This recipe makes about 2 cups (500 ml) of ghee. Note: Use either one 12-in (30-cm) square piece of fine muslin or four layers of cheesecloth.

Lentils *see* Dried Legumes

Mangoes This fruit is native to the Indian sub-continent, where it has been grown for more than 4,000 years. Because the mango seed can't be dispersed naturally by wind or water, owing to its large size and weight, it is believed that people who moved from one region to another transported the fruit to new areas. Though mango cultivation has now spread to many parts of the tropical and sub-tropical world, including Brazil, Mexico, the West Indies, and parts of Florida, nearly half of the world's mangoes are cultivated in India alone.

Mangoes are widely used in Indian cuisine. The green, unripe mangoes are sour and are used to make chutneys, pickles, and sometimes side dishes such as Chickpea, Mango, and Watercress Salad (page 45). As a chef's tip, I say when you make salads calling for a crunchy vegetable like carrots or radishes, replace them with green, unripe mangoes for a unique tangy twist. Green, unripe mangoes are also eaten raw with a sprinkle of salt and Asian red chili powder or cayenne pepper, which is my favorite way to eat them. Chilled Mango Cooler (page 132), a very popular and refreshing summer drink, is made with green, unripe mangoes blended with water, mint, sugar, salt, cumin, and ice.

Ripe mangoes are typically eaten fresh. Mango Lassi (page 133), made by adding mango pulp to yogurt, is the most popular drink in India and Indian restaurants worldwide. Ripe mangoes are used to make desserts as well as savory curries. Aamras—sweetened, thick, ripe mango pulp with the flavor of cardamom—is a popular dish in western India that is served along with Fried Puffed Bread (page 125). The Alfonso mango is considered the sweetest and best of all the eating mangoes. For some recipes, I use canned Alfonso mango purée (available in Indian grocery stores) when fresh ones are not in season.

When shopping for ripe mangoes, look for fruit with unblemished yellow skin with a red tinge or blush. You should avoid mangoes that have bruises or soft spots. You can buy green mangoes and ripen them at home by placing them in a brown paper bag on your counter for a week. Ripe mangoes will last 2–3 days at room temperature or for up to 5 days in a plastic bag in the refrigerator.

You can find green mangoes in most Indian, Southeast Asian, or South American markets. When shopping for green mangoes, make sure they are firm and their skins are dark green in color and unblemished. Store them at room temperature uncovered. They will last about 2 weeks.

Mint An aromatic, almost exclusively perennial herb with a very refreshing taste, fresh mint is used in Indian marinades, chutneys, drinks, and desserts and in curries and rice dishes. I also use dried mint for making breads in my kitchen. Chopped fresh mint leaves steeped in a cup of hot water with tea and honey is one of my favorite after-dinner beverages. The spearmint variety is most commonly used in Indian cooking. When purchasing mint, make sure the leaves are fresh and green in color without black spots or cracks. See "Storage Tips for Spices and Herbs," page 12.

Mustard Seeds These tiny, round, hot and pungent seeds are from an annual plant in the cabbage family. They are available in white, yellow, brown, or black colors. The white seeds, the largest type, are used to make commercial mustards in the United States; the yellow and brown seeds are used for European mustards and for pickling. In India, the black seeds are used in cooking and are the source of commonly used oil. Black mustard seeds are used whole and in powdered form. The whole seeds are used in vegetables dishes, curries, appetizers, salads, and dried legumes, while the powder is used to flavor steamed fish, pickles, and, again, curries. Mustard seeds are available at Indian grocery stores and online (see Shopping Guide, page 140).

Oils and Fats In Indian kitchens, oil is used alone or in combination with ghee (clarified butter) to fry flavorings at the start of cooking or to deep-fry foods. The oil used depends on the culture and region. When I call for oil, you may use any neutral-flavored vegetable oil (for example, canola, safflower, or corn oil). In addition to using unflavored oils, Indians use toasted sesame oil, coconut oil, and peanut and mustard oils to impart distinct flavors to dishes.

I have not used these oils in my recipes because some are hard to find and they give a very distinct flavor to the food, which, though popular in India, can be an acquired taste for non-Indians. When I call for oil for deep-frying, it's important to use an oil that is relatively stable at high temperatures, such as peanut or safflower oil. Olive oil, which is a very healthy oil, can also be used to cook Indian food.

Paprika Known as *kashmiri mirch* in India, paprika is a red powder made from dried, mild, non-pungent chili peppers. It is mainly used for the rich red hue it adds to curries. When added to hot oil, it immediately releases a deep red color. Most Indian paprika comes from Kashmir, hence the name. Kashmiri mirch is available at Indian grocery stores or online (see Shopping Guide, page 140). The easily available, mild Hungarian paprika is a good substitute.

Peppercorns These are one of the oldest-known spices and are often referred to as the king of spices. Peppercorns are the berries of the pepper plant, a branching evergreen creeper that grows mainly in the hot and humid monsoon forests of southwest India. The plant is indigenous to India and dates back to 4,000 BCE. The very

tangy, slightly hot berries grow like clusters of grapes on the pepper plant. Peppercorns range in color from white to green to black. White peppercorns are picked ripe, and their outer skin is removed. Green peppercorns are underripe berries that are cured in brine. Black peppercorns are picked underripe and allowed to dry until dark black. Black peppercorns are most commonly used and impart an incredible flavor to all curries. The world's top quality black pepper is grown in Indian in the southwest coastal state of Kerala and is known as Tellicherry pepper. The recipes in this book call for dry and oil-roasted, ground and crushed black peppercorns.

Pulses *see* Dried Legumes

Rice is an indispensable part of Indian meals. It is served as a staple alongside curries and dals and is eaten at least twice a day in India. There are many distinctive kinds of rice grown and sold in the Indian subcontinent. For everyday meals, the type of rice used varies from region to region. While people in southern regions prefer the locally available red rice or long-grain variety, northerners prefer aromatic Basmati rice, which grows in the foothills of the Himalayas.

One of my favorite varieties of rice,

which I grew up eating, is medium-grain parboiled rice known as "red boiled rice" or "rosematta rice." It is made by parboiling the rice before husking. After parboiling, the grain is separated from the husk, thereby leaving a part of the bran on the grain and giving the rice its red or reddish-brown color. It can then be boiled like any other form of rice, though it takes twice as long to cook and often requires more water. I have not used it in this book because it is only available at Indian grocery stores or online. If you do run across it and would like to try it, I recommend serving it with dishes from the southwest of India, and in particular with Kerala-Style Chicken Stew (page 94) and Goan-Style Mackerel (page 89).

Basmati, which means "queen of fragrance" in Hindi, is the most popular and the best-known rice of India, and the most expensive. It has a wonderful fragrance when cooked with whole spices and is a good match for all Indian dishes. Basmati rice is always used for *puloas* and *biriyanis*—two types of rice dishes—for it absorbs flavors beautifully and yet keeps its shape during cooking. Basmati rice, though preferred, is not absolutely necessary for simpler rice preparations, such as Lemon Rice with Peanuts (page 114) or Coconut Rice (page 112). Whereas Basmati rice needs to be soaked prior to being rinsed and drained, ordinary long-grain rice only needs to be rinsed and drained.

Rosewater or rose syrup is the leftover liquid remaining when rose petals and water are distilled together. It imparts an intoxicating fragrance of roses to rice

dishes, desserts, and drinks. Considered very auspicious for its aroma, it is also diluted with water and sprinkled at various religious and cultural ceremonies in India. A teaspoonful may be added to desserts like Milk Dumplings in Saffron Syrup (page 129), and drinks like Mango Lassi (page 133), meat dishes like Lamb Shank Korma (page 104), or to rice dishes to create a unique taste and aroma. It is available in Indian or Middle Eastern grocery stores.

Saffron These intense yellow-orange threads are the dried, orange to deep-red stigmas of the small, purple saffron crocus flower, a member of the iris family. It is the world's most expensive spice as it takes almost 75,000 handpicked blossoms to make one pound of saffron. Use saffron sparingly as it just takes four to five strands to flavor a dish that feeds four. It has a distinctly warm, rich, powerful, and intense flavor. It is available in strands or ground. I recommend the strands for the sake of more assured quality. Gently heat saffron on a dry skillet before using, as heat brings out its aroma. There is no acceptable substitute for saffron. It is available in Indian or Middle Eastern grocery stores, gourmet stores, and online (see Shopping Guide, page 140).

Salt The most common salt in North America is table salt. It is very fine in texture and is often supplemented with iodine. Table salt, when compared to kosher or sea salt, is much "saltier." Sea salt is the most popular salt in Indian cooking. Measurements used in the recipes in this book are for common table salt. If you prefer kosher or sea salt, you will most likely need to increase the amount by 10 to 15 percent. However, it is always a good idea to taste and check for seasoning before adding more. **Black Salt** *kala namak* Contrary to its name, powdered black salt is purplish pink. It is an unrefined sea salt with a very strong and sulfurous taste. It is available in rock or powder form and is very traditional to India. Its distinctive, earthy flavor and aroma help to bring out the flavor in relishes, salads, *raitas*, and snacks. It is an essential ingredient in making Chaat Masala (page 22). Black salt is a better choice for those on a low-sodium diet because of its lower sodium content. It is available in Indian grocery stores. Feel adventurous? Try sprinkling ¼ teaspoon of black salt, a pinch of black pepper, and squeeze of fresh lime to a chilled glass of Pepsi or Coke to enjoy a masala cola, a popular Indian street-style summer drink.

Star Anise This dried, star-shaped, dark-brown pod contains licorice-flavored seeds. The pods grow on an evergreen tree that is a member of the magnolia family. Star anise is used to flavor and add an enticing aroma to both sweet and savory dishes. It is often used on its own or ground with different spices to make blends. This spice is available at Indian and Asian grocery stores, online (see Shopping Guide, page 140), and at many conventional supermarkets.

Sesame Seeds These tiny seeds are harvested from a flowering plant that grows widely in tropical regions around the world and is cultivated for its edible seeds. Whole or ground white sesame seeds are used in savory Indian dishes, breads, and many sweets. Sometimes the seeds are toasted to heighten their nutty flavor. They come in a host of different colors, depending on the variety, including white, yellow, black, and red. In general, the paler varieties of sesame are used in the West and Middle East, while the black varieties are more common in the East. They are available in most grocery stores.

Tamarind This is the curved, brown bean pod of the tamarind tree. The pod contains a sticky pulp enclosing one to twelve shiny black seeds. It is the pulp that is used as a flavoring for its sweet-and-sour fruity aroma and taste. It is used in chutneys, preserves, and curries. Tamarind is available in South Asian grocery stores, natural foods stores, and some conventional supermarkets in one or more of the following three ways: in pod form; pressed into a fibrous dried slab; and in jars of tamarind "paste" or "concentrate," which has a jam-like consistency. I use the tamarind paste in the recipes in this book simply because it is the most convenient form to use and is fairly easy to find.

Alternatively, to create tamarind juice from the dried slab, soak a walnut-size chunk of the dried pulp (this is equivalent to 1 teaspoon tamarind paste) in ½ cup (125 ml) of warm water for 15 minutes. After soaking the pulp in water, break it up with your fingers and then mash it with a fork until the liquid is muddy brown in appearance. Strain this mixture before use through a fine-mesh strainer. Using the back of spoon, mash and push the pulp through the fine-mesh strainer to extract any remaining juice.

Turmeric It is a rhizome of a tropical plant in the ginger family. The fresh root is boiled, peeled, sun-dried, and ground into a bright yellow-orange powder. Ground turmeric has a warm, peppery aroma—reminiscent of ginger—and a strong, bitter taste that mellows with cooking. It is used to color many curries or as a "poor man's substitute" for saffron since it imparts a similar color; the taste, however, is quite different.

Yogurt Thick and creamy yogurt is made every day in homes across the Indian subcontinent and it is an important part of every meal. It is most commonly enjoyed plain as a mild contrast to spicy foods. Raitas—cooling salads made with yogurt and crunchy vegetables—are very popular. Yogurt is often churned into cooling drinks with spices and is the base for many desserts. In savory cooking, its main role is as a souring agent, though it also aids digestion. In India it is customary to end a meal with either plain yogurt mixed with rice or a glass of Indian spiced "buttermilk" (thinned yogurt with salt, green chilies, ginger, and salt) common in south India. The best yogurt for the recipes in this book is a thick, plain, natural yogurt made from whole milk. Look for organic, whole-milk yogurt for the best consistency and flavor.

Chapter 1 THE BASICS

Most Indian meals are prepared fresh. But it makes your cooking easier and less stressful if you have a few basic preparations and key ingredients made up in advance. If you understand the basic preparations and techniques, know your way around the kitchen, and have a love of good food, you can master Indian cooking. Don't hesitate to experiment with spices, as the discoveries made can be very flavorful and rewarding.

Indian cooking is all about spices and flavor. To the Indian cook, the two are one and the same: spice equals flavor. To understand Indian cooking is to understand how to use spices individually and in combination to enhance food. The specific mixture of spices in the food is referred to as a *masala*, which means a blend of spices or herbs. It is this unique combination of spices or herbs that creates the distinctive taste of each dish. This section includes recipes for masalas and other basic flavor components that form the building blocks of Indian cooking.

Masalas can be in the form of a powder or a paste. Different Indian recipes may call for a different blend of masalas in either form. Often a recipe will call for a just a sprinkling of mustard seeds and ground turmeric, whereas some recipes may call for a masala that is a blend of many different spices. In fact, even a minimal use of spices will lend a wonderful, aromatic accent to a dish. So do not hesitate to use just a few spices to create your masalas.

The proportion of ingredients in these spice blends, as well as the amount used in a recipe, can be adjusted to suit your taste. Experiment by tweaking the spice profiles to arrive at your own personal versions. You can also substitute many of these masalas with store-bought, prepared spice mixes. However, for the best flavor, I recommend using freshly blended spices. When making masalas at home, you are able to slightly roast the spices before grinding them into a powder or a paste—an extra step that helps release the flavors and oils of spices into the blend, thus adding more potency (and magic!) to the spice mixture.

Café Spice Garam Masala

Garam masala, literally "hot spice," is the most popular spice blend used in Indian cooking. It is the basic essence of Indian cooking. There are as many versions of garam masala as there are chefs. This recipe blend is what I use very often in my kitchen. It is important that the spices are blended fresh as needed. Many store-bought garam masala blends aren't roasted and tend to be very poor in flavor. Try this recipe and you will never buy a ready-made version.

Prep time: **5 minutes**
Cook time: **5 minutes**
Makes about **⅔ cup (75 g)**

2 tablespoons cumin seeds
1 tablespoon coriander seeds
1 tablespoon black peppercorns
1 dried red chili pepper
10 dried allspice berries
1 stick cinnamon, ½-in (1.25-cm)
10 green cardamom pods
1 teaspoon whole cloves
1 teaspoon fennel seeds
5 bay leaves

In a small skillet, dry roast the whole spices over medium heat, stirring until fragrant, 1–2 minutes. Remove the spices from the skillet and set aside to let cool completely. Grind the spices in an electric spice grinder to a fine powder and store in an airtight jar for up to 4–6 weeks.

Chaat Masala

Chaat is a commonly used term to describe street snacks of India. These small dishes are infused with a complex blend of sweet, tangy, and spicy flavors. They are always seasoned with a spice mix called *chaat masala*. Like any other Indian spice blend, each one has its own regional variation throughout India. This spice blend is great for more than just snacks. You can use it to jazz up your salads, dressings, fresh fruit, fruit juices, and grilled meats. This spice blend is easily available pre-mixed at Indian grocery stores.

Prep time: **5 minutes**
Cook time: **5 minutes**
Makes about **1½ cups (200 g)**

1 tablespoon cumin seeds, roasted and ground
4 tablespoons dried green mango powder (*amchoor*)
2 tablespoons ginger powder
2 tablespoons ground *ajwain* seeds (optional)
1 tablespoon finely ground sea salt, preferably black salt (*kala namak*) or 2 teaspoons common table salt
2 teaspoons Asian red chili powder
1 teaspoon ground asafetida (optional)

In a medium, nonstick skillet, dry roast the ingredients, stirring and shaking the pan over medium heat, until heated through, about 2–3 minutes. Remove the spices from the skillet and set aside to let cool completely. Store in an airtight container. The shelf life is about 1 month at room temperature or it will last about 6 months if it is stored in the refrigerator.

NOTE ABOUT THE INGREDIENTS—
Amchoor is a green mango powder. Unripe, sour green mangoes are sliced and dried in the sun and then ground. Amchoor, a key ingredient in chaat masala, is one of the many souring agents used in Indian cooking. *Ajwain*, sometimes called *carom*, is a small, grayish, egg-shaped spice. It is commonly used in Indian cuisine. Raw ajwain smells almost exactly like thyme, however, it is more aromatic and less subtle in taste, as well as slightly bitter and pungent. It is only available in stores as a whole seed. Amchoor and ajwain are available at Indian grocery stores, specialty stores, or online (see Shopping Guide, page 140).

Ginger-Garlic Paste

Although you can easily find ginger-garlic pastes at Asian markets, it is simple enough to make it at home and it keeps well in the refrigerator. Plus the homemade paste gives the dish a much better flavor than the store-bought one. Basically it is just equal amounts of fresh ginger and garlic pulsed together.

Makes about **1½ cups (500 g)**

2 pieces ginger (about 8 oz/250 g), each about 4 in (10 cm) in length, peeled and coarsely chopped
½ lb (250 g) garlic (about 6–7 heads), coarsely chopped
¼ cup (65 ml) water

Place the ginger and garlic in a food processor or a blender. Add the water and process to make a fine paste. Store the paste in a clean jar with a tight-fitting lid in the refrigerator up to 3–4 weeks.

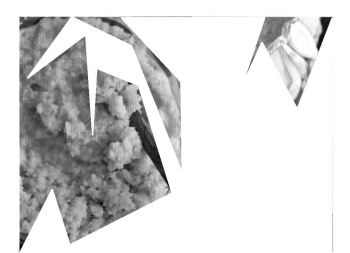

Indian Curry Basics and Tips

Unlike in Western cooking, flour is almost never used to thicken Indian sauces and curries. The dark, thick sauces in Indian cooking are achieved through a proper balance of ingredients and correct cooking techniques. For example, the body of Indian sauces very often comes from onions, garlic, ginger, and tomatoes, which may be chopped, creating a textured sauce, or made into a paste in a food processor or a blender. Once a paste is made, it is then cooked or browned in oil. The sauce is allowed to cook further until it is reduced and becomes thick. Sometimes cream, yogurt, coconut, or nut pastes such as those from almonds and cashews are added to Indian sauces to give a creamy texture.

SIMPLE HOMESTYLE CURRY

CHICKEN CURRY— 1 lb (500 g)
  Cornish hen, or 2 breast fillets,
  or 4 thighs, or 6 drumsticks
LAMB CURRY— 10 oz (300 g)
  stewing diced lamb
FISH CURRY— 2 fillets of cod,
  about 8 oz, or 2 salmon steaks
VEGETABLE CURRY— 8 oz seasonal
  mixed diced vegetables
4 tablespoons oil
1 large onion (about 8 oz/250 g),
  minced
1 tablespoon Ginger-Garlic Paste
  (page 22)
½ teaspoon ground coriander
¼ teaspoon ground turmeric
¼ teaspoon ground cumin
¼ teaspoon Café Spice Garam
  Masala (page 22)
1 teaspoon Asian red chili powder
  or cayenne pepper
2 tomatoes (about 8 oz/250 g),
  chopped
Salt, to taste
2 tablespoons
  leaves (cila

Heat the oil in a heavy saucepan over medium heat. Add the onion and sauté for about 10–15 minutes or until deep brown (browning). Add the Ginger-Garlic Paste and fry for 1 minute. Add the ground coriander and stir for a further full minute. Then add the turmeric, cumin, garam masala, Asian red chili powder or cayenne powder, and sauté for 30 seconds (*bhunao*). Add 1 cup (250 ml) of water and cook for 10 minutes. Put in the tomatoes, stir well, and cook for 5 more minutes. Add salt, to taste.

Add in the chicken, lamb, fish, or vegetables. Add 1½ cups of water for the chicken, 2½ cups (625 ml) for the lamb, 1 cup (250 ml) for the fish, and 2 cups (500 ml) for the vegetables. Cook until done. Sprinkle with chopped coriander leaves just before serving.

CHEF'S TIPS

- Indian cooking tends to have many ingredients. Prepare all the ingredients before you begin to cook. Keep the spices handy by the stove.
- If cooking for a special event, you can cook the sauce, marinate the meat, cook the lentils ahead of time, and finish the dish before serving. Vegetables can be cut and set aside, a day in advance. Bread dough can be made a day ahead. Chutneys and accompaniments can be made a day ahead and stored in an airtight container in the fridge. Curries of meat and chicken can be frozen. Cooked lentils, chickpeas, and vegetables freeze well.
- Always keep Ginger-Garlic Paste ready in your refrigerator; it will come in handy. Browned onions must be fried in batches and refrigerated or frozen.
- Most of the recipes call for fresh tomatoes. Canned tomato purée sometimes replac
  but the
  won't b

- If onions burn while browning, remove the burnt bits, change the pot, and add a little fresh oil. If a burnt taste persists, you will have to start again.
- If the dish has become too spicy and contains tomatoes and/or whipped yogurt, or coconut milk, add an extra tomato or two. Also add ½ -1 teaspoon of sugar. Adding sourness sometimes helps to cut down the heat. On the other hand if the dish is not spicy enough, fry some chopped green chili peppers in hot oil in a small saucepan and add it to the dish.
- If the curry has become too salty, add pieces of potato, which you must remove before serving. The potatoes will absorb the liquid and then you can top up with a cup of plain water to dilute the saltiness.
- If the sauce is too liquid, boil uncovered for a few extra minutes, until it reaches the desired consistency.

Chapter 2 CHUTNEYS AND ACCOMPANIMENTS

Similar in preparation and usage to pickles, simple spiced chutneys, as they are referred to in India, can be dated as far back as 500 BCE. Originating in Northern Europe, this method of preserving food was subsequently adopted by the Romans and later by the British empire which exported this technique to its colonies, Australia and America. The first chutneys that arrived in India would have been sticky, fruit-based preserves. Chutneys add that little "something extra" to every bite of a meal. A different word *achar* (pickle) applies to preserves that often contain oil and are rarely sweet. Vinegar or citrus juice may be added as natural preservatives, or fermentation in the presence of salt may be used to create acid. Traditionally, chutneys are ground with a mortar and pestle made of stone. Spices are added and ground, usually in a particular order; the resulting wet paste is sautéed in vegetable oil.

There are also *raita*s—the most common and popular Indian accompaniment—which act as a coolant for curries and other fiery-hot Indian dishes. A raita is a simple preparation made by adding fruits, vegetables, or any other thing to beaten curds. Most Indian families enjoy curds either plain or in the form of delicious raitas as an accompaniment with lunch or dinner. Raitas are unique because they are cool and spicy at the same time. A delectable cross between a sauce and a dip, they act as a digestive element. Some are even cooked and tempered to give them a different dimension.

No Indian meal is complete without at least one accompaniment, and fancy meals may have five or more. Additionally, this is one element that can be played around with, without any remorse or regret. You can use regular vegetables like peas or carrots; use readily available dips like mayonnaise to flavor; or add a twist of magic into a raita with a dash of any Indian spice, for example, mustard or fenugreek. Although I have suggested a few sample dishes where these accompaniments can be used, I urge you to trust your culinary instincts wherever possible and try experimenting with seasonal fresh fruit or other produce, basic spices, and herbs that are readily available at the market.

In India, chutneys are usually freshly made each day. However, they preserve well. I often make them in batches and save them up for when I need that extra zing of flavor.

Spiced Pear Chutney Nasapati Ki Chutney

Chutneys made with fruits are becoming popular in markets in the West as well as in boutique organic food stores. The sweet fruits of summer—peaches, plums, apples, and pears—are simmered with tangy vinegar, sugar, and spices to make this delicious version of chutney. Once you make a big batch of this, it is one of the finest preserves to keep in your cupboard year round. The chutney adds its mildly piquant and exotic note to creamy cheese on bread and crackers or to cold meats and curries. Another exciting idea is to store them in pretty bottles and give them as gifts on holidays like Thanksgiving and Christmas.

Makes about 2 cups (500 g)
Prep time: 15 minutes
Cook time: 35 minutes

3 tablespoons oil
5 dried red chili peppers, broken into pieces
1½ teaspoons fennel seeds
1 teaspoon cumin seeds
¼ cup (25 g) dried fenugreek leaves (optional)
½ teaspoon paprika

¼ teaspoon asafetida (optional)
6 Bartlett or Anjou pears (about 3½ lbs/ 1.5 kg), peeled, cored, quartered, and diced
1½ teaspoons kosher salt
¼ cup (50 g) sugar
2 tablespoons white wine vinegar

Heat the oil in a large saucepan over medium heat. Add the chilies, fennel seeds, and cumin seeds, stirring until the spices are slightly roasted and aromatic. Stir in the fenugreek leaves (if using), paprika, and asafetida (if using) and cook for another 30 seconds.

Add the pears and cook until the they get juicy, about 3–4 minutes.

Stir in the salt, sugar, and vinegar. Reduce the heat to medium and cook, stirring often, until the pears are soft, sticky, and deeply golden and caramelized, 30–40 minutes. Once cooled, transfer to a plastic container and refrigerate for up to 1 week or ladle into dry and sterilized jars.

Tamarind Chutney

Tamarind Chutney   Imli Chutney

This basic chutney is readily available in most kitchens in the Indian home. It is served with chaats and samosas, and closer to home, you can serve it with a huge bowl of French fries or with various fritters. The addition of dates makes it thicker and gives it some coarse texture, rather than leaving it as a smooth sauce. The shelf life of this chutney is very long, so make a big batch and store it in bottles in your pantry.

Makes **about 1¼ cups (300 g)**
Prep time: **15 minutes**
Cook time: **35 minutes**

1 tablespoon oil
1 teaspoon cumin seeds
½ teaspoon fennel seeds
½ teaspoon Asian red chili powder or cayenne pepper
½ teaspoon asafetida (optional)
½ teaspoon Café Spice Garam Masala (page 22)
2½ cups (625 ml) water
1¼ cups (250 g) sugar
Salt, to taste
½ cup (60 g) dates, pitted chopped
3 tablespoons tamarind paste

In a medium saucepan, heat the oil over medium heat. Add the cumin seeds, fennel seeds, chili powder, asafetida, and Garam Masala. Cook until the spices are fragrant and lightly toasted, about 30–40 seconds.

Whisk in the water, sugar, salt, dates, and tamarind paste until completely dissolved and bring to a boil. Turn the heat down to medium and simmer until the sauce turns thick enough to leave a trail on the back of a spoon, 20–30 minutes.

Take it off the flame, cool slightly, and use a hand blender to blend it to a smooth purée.

When it's cold, transfer to a covered plastic container and store in the refrigerator for up to 2 weeks or ladle into dry and sterilized jars and can according to the manufacturer's instructions.

Mint Chutney   Pudina Chutney

This is one of the signature collection in the Café Spice repertoire. It is an immense hit and among the most popular accompaniments. We make it fresh every day and serve it to our delighted customers, who often ask us how it is made so tasty! Here is the closest version of the secret recipe—just for you! This versatile chutney can be used as a condiment, dip, or even as a spread. When buying fresh mint, look for bright green sturdy stems and leaves with a characteristic mint fragrance.

Makes **1 cup (250 g)**
Prep time: **10 minutes**

2–4 medium fresh green chili peppers
2 cups (80 g) packed fresh mint leaves
1 cup (40 g) packed fresh coriander leaves (cilantro)
4 tablespoons fresh lime juice
¼ cup (65 ml) water
1 teaspoon sugar
Salt, to taste

In a food processor or a blender, process the chili peppers, mint, and coriander leaves until minced. Scrape the sides with a spatula. As you process, drizzle in the fresh lime juice and water and process until the chutney is smooth. Add the sugar and salt. Taste and adjust the seasonings if needed. Transfer to a bowl and serve immediately or refrigerate for future use.

Peanut and Garlic Chutney
Moong-Phali aur Lassan Ki Chutney

This chutney is usually served with wholesome meals called *thali*s in southern India. A thali contains several small portions of various dishes, complete with relishes and sweets. The thalis of south India use this chutney as part of their meal. For a more contemporary usage, you can also make this and serve it as a topping or dip with grilled chicken/meat skewers or any appetizers. The peanuts create a very crunchy texture that makes it delicious. The coconut, an optional ingredient, adds to the creaminess of the finished chutney.

Serves 4
Prep time: 5 minutes
Cook time: 5 minutes

2 tablespoons vegetable oil
1¾ cups (180 g) skinned peanuts
½ teaspoon Asian red chili powder or cayenne pepper
3 cloves garlic, roughly chopped
½-in (1.25-cm) piece fresh ginger, roughly chopped
2 dried red chili peppers, roughly chopped
1 teaspoon salt
1 teaspoon sugar
4 tablespoons coconut milk (optional) or 2 tablespoons shredded unsweetened coconut
   (frozen, reconstituted, or freshly grated)
Juice of 1 lemon

Heat the oil in a skillet, add the peanuts, and fry until golden.
Remove from the heat and leave to cool.
Put all the ingredients in a food processor and blend to a paste.
Check the seasoning and serve at room temperature.

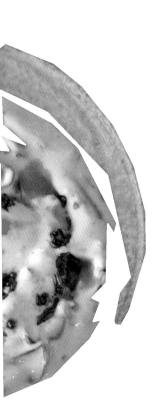

Spinach and Tomato Raita Palak aur Tamatar Raita

This *raita* makes for a great table accompaniment. It can be served with *chapati* or a dry chicken or meat preparation for a meal. Spinach is not only a good source of iron, which is where much of its health benefit lies, but is also quick to prepare and makes the dish fresh, green, and ideal for a weekday summer meal spread that balances out any spicy main course dish.

Serves 4
Prep time: 15 minutes
Cook time: 5 minutes

½ lb (250 g) fresh spinach leaves
1 tablespoon vegetable oil
1 teaspoon cumin seeds
1 teaspoon mustard seeds
2 cups (500 g), plain yogurt, whisked until smooth
1 small tomato (about 4 oz/125 g), chopped
½ teaspoon Asian red chili powder or cayenne pepper
Salt, to taste
Freshly ground black pepper, to taste
1 tablespoon freshly squeezed lemon juice

Bring a large pan of salted water to a boil, add the spinach and blanch for 30–40 seconds. Drain through a colander and refresh under running cold water. With the spinach still in the colander, press down the back of a large spoon or ladle to squeeze out the excess moisture. Pat the spinach dry with paper towels, then lay the leaves out on a chopping board and chop finely.

Heat the oil in a small skillet and place over medium heat. Add the cumin and mustard seeds and fry for 20 seconds or until the seeds begin to pop and splutter. Pour the oil and seeds into a small bowl and leave to cool.

Add the chopped spinach, cumin, mustard seeds, and chili powder into the whisked yogurt. Season with salt, black pepper, and lemon juice and keep chilled until ready to serve.

Serves 4
Prep time: **10 minutes**
Cook time: **2 minutes**

2 cups (300 g) green peas, fresh or frozen
1-in (2.5-cm) piece fresh ginger, roughly
    chopped
3 cloves garlic, roughly chopped
2 fresh green chili peppers, roughly chopped
½ teaspoon salt
½ teaspoon sugar
1½ tablespoons olive oil
½ teaspoon mustard seeds
10 fresh curry leaves
Juice of ½ lime

Place the peas, ginger, garlic, green chilies, salt,
    sugar, and 1 tablespoon of the olive oil in a food
    processor and blend it to a smooth purée.
Transfer to a bowl.
Heat the remaining olive oil in a small pan, add the
    mustard seeds and curry leaves, and let them
    crackle.
Remove from the heat and pour the mixture over the
    pea purée.
Check the seasoning and finish with the lime juice.

Green Pea Relish Matar Ki Chutney

Green pea is quite an unconventional ingredient to use in a relish, particularly in light of the belief that green chutney can only be made with mint and coriander leaves. But this recipe will convert you! You will find verdant pods of fresh peas in farmers' markets all through spring and summer. Buy them in bulk and you can even store the shelled peas for later. This chutney can be used as a table accompaniment for any meal or even used as a seafood or pasta sauce as a substitute for the traditional salsa verde. Keep it chunkier and it marries very well with any white fish preparation.

Lentil and Sprout Relish   Dal aur Phooti Mung ka Salaad

Sprouting is a time-consuming process, but for most of us, it is worth every effort, just because of the health benefits. You need to soak the beans overnight, drain off all the water, rinse, and allow some air to circulate into the rinsed beans. Only then will the beans germinate or sprout. An easier alternative is to buy them already sprouted at the grocery store. This recipe uses green gram (mung beans), which is always the best option. This dish is a favorite among weight watchers. You can add a few more ingredients to convert it into a wholesome salad or make it a delicious, healthy meal by adding dried fruits, walnuts, apples, carrots, or even spinach leaves.

Serves 4
Prep time: **15 minutes**
Cook time: **15 minutes**

½ **cup (50 g) sprouted green gram (moong dal)**
½ **cup (100 g) split yellow peas (chana dal), soaked**
    overnight and boiled until tender
2 **cucumbers (about 8 oz/250 g), peeled, seeded, and**
    chopped
¼ **cup (10 g) fresh coriander leaves (cilantro),**
    chopped
1 **fresh green chili pepper, seeded and finely chopped**
Juice of 1 lemon
½ **teaspoon salt**
1 **teaspoon oil**
¼ **teaspoon black mustard seeds**
1 **tablespoon plain yogurt**

Mix together the sprouted green gram, split yellow peas,
    cucumber, fresh coriander leaves, lemon juice, and salt
    in a large mixing bowl. Set aside.
Heat the oil in a small skillet over medium heat and add
    the mustard seeds. When they splutter, take the pan off
    the heat and stir in the yogurt. Add this mixture to the
    salad and toss well. Serve immediately.

Pumpkin Pickle Kaddu ka Achaar

This is one of those recipes that I produced from memory after I first had a taste of it at the Malhotra family's house. It is Sushil's mother-in-law, Durupadi Jagtiani's recipe. I can still remember the first bite of this pickle: the tartness of a sour ingredient that was so well complemented by the sweetness of the red pumpkin and the heat of the red chilies. Although this recipe uses dried mango powder (popularly known as *amchoor* in India), lime juice can be an easy substitute.

Serves 4
Prep time: 5 minutes
Cook time: 15 minutes

4 tablespoons vegetable oil
½ teaspoon fenugreek seeds
4 dried red chili peppers, broken into 2–3 pieces each
1 lb 9 oz (700 g) peeled pumpkin flesh, cut into ½-in (1.25-cm) dice
2 teaspoons salt
1 tablespoon Asian red chili powder or cayenne pepper
1 teaspoon ground turmeric
5 tablespoons sugar
2 teaspoons dried green mango powder (amchoor, optional)

Heat the oil in a pan, add the fenugreek seeds and dried red chilies, and let them pop.
Add the pumpkin and stir over a high heat for 3–4 minutes.
Stir in the salt, chili powder, and turmeric. Then reduce the heat, cover, and cook until the pumpkin is soft and begins to break down.
Stir in the sugar—the sweetness balances the heat and spice and also makes the pickle glossy.
Finish with the dried mango powder, if using.

South Indian Cabbage Slaw
Kosu Pachdhi

Coleslaw is one of the most common accompaniments and it is often used as a salad in American recipes. This version has a spice twist that gives it an Indian flavor. It can be used on sandwiches, hotdogs, or burgers and even served as an accompaniment to grilled and baked entrees. An interesting option that can be used instead of mayonnaise is yogurt, which gives an equivalent creamy texture, minus all the calories! Additionally, the yogurt and the Indian spices in this recipe go very well together.

Serves 4
Prep time: 15 minutes
Cook time: 2 minutes

¼ head cabbage (about 4 oz/125 g), shredded
1 medium carrot, peeled and grated (about 1 cup/100 g)
¼ cup (25 g) shredded unsweetened coconut (frozen, reconstituted, or freshly grated)
Juice of 1 lime
1 fresh green chili pepper, minced
½ teaspoon sugar
½ teaspoon salt
2 tablespoons oil
¼ teaspoon mustard seeds
¼ teaspoon cumin seeds
8–10 curry leaves
½ cup (125 g) yogurt

Mix the shredded cabbage, carrots, and shredded coconut in a bowl.
Whisk the lime juice, green chili, sugar, and salt in a small bowl. Pour this dressing over the cabbage mixture and toss well.
Heat the oil in a small pan, add the mustard and cumin seeds, and when they pop, add the curry leaves and yogurt. Remove from the heat and mix with the cabbage and carrot mixture. Transfer to a serving dish and serve cold.

Chapter 3 STARTERS AND SALADS

Salads hold many of the essential nutrients the body needs and are very good for general health. Hence, a dinner is incomplete without salad. They are delicious, healthy, and easy to make as well. Salads are used to enhance the main course of the meal. The good thing about having salads on a menu containing Indian food is that they often help to balance the spice and the heat of the masalas used in other foods. Indian salads can be dry or yogurt-based, raw or cooked. Vegetables like cucumber, carrot, onion, tomatoes, and sprouts are usually used.

Salads in an everyday Indian home are often quite unimaginative. A few basic fresh vegetables like the carrot, cucumber, tomatoes, and onions are sliced or chopped, dressed with salt, pepper, and lemon juice and served along with everyday meals. Here in the West, we have a slight advantage because we have access to ingredients that aren't typically Indian, but have the potential to merge delightfully with Indian spices and flavors. Typically, salads are served with the meal rather than as a separate course. Feel free to mix fresh seasonal fruits and vegetables with homemade dressings of yogurt, lemon juice, and freshly ground Indian spices.

Indian cuisine has a rich array of appetizers, snacks, and hors d'oeuvres. Unlike most Western appetizers, which are heavy on butter and cheese, many Indian appetizers are relatively low in fat. Most Indian street-food—from *bhajias* (deep-fried, battered veggies) to samosas (pastry with delicious fillings) and kebabs—ends up as an appetizer when recreated and presented on a plate.

Appetizers like Potato and Pea Samosas (page 46), Shrimp Stuffed Pappadum (page 42) or Veggie Sloppy Joe (page 36) may be served either before the meal or at tea time with a cup of steaming hot chai. In most Indian families, tea time is in the early evening or late afternoon, with dinner following a few hours later. Indians can never get enough of spicy appetizers and snacks. Indians are social and gather around for any excuse to catch a lively conversation and share a plate of snacks. These snacks go well with our other favorite pastime—drinking tea! Most Indian appetizers can be served with mint, coriander, tamarind or coconut chutney, or any of the accompaniments mentioned in this book. Some can be used as dips, and some can be simply dolloped over these appetizers.

Veggie Sloppy Joe Pau Bhaji

This is my take on the popular Indian street food, Pau Bhaji, that is sold in carts that dot the side of every alternate lane in the city of Mumbai. Even within the city, there are variations in the taste. I like to make the *bhaji* (filling) not so mashed up that I can't see what I'm eating. This preparation style also provides a nice texture and leaves some crunch to the veggies. In America, the closest parallel to this dish is the sloppy joe that is usually made with wet, seasoned minced meat spooned over a bun. The Indian sloppy joe uses a lot of butter to gives it its characteristic taste. You can use any vegetable for this recipe. In fact, feel free to also try out the various pau bhaji masalas that are now readily available in your Indian grocery. Add that to mashed veggies, place it between a burger bun or sandwich bread, and you can have a quick meal-to-go!

Serves 4
Prep time: 25 minutes, plus 15 minutes for
    cooling
Cooking time: 20 minutes

5 potatoes (about 2½ lbs/1 kg)
2 tomatoes (about 12 oz/360 g) chopped
1 cup (130 g) green peas, fresh or frozen
    (shelled from 1 lb/500 g fresh pea pods
    or about half a 10 oz/300 g package of
    frozen peas
3½ oz (100 g) butter or ghee, plus extra to
    serve (optional)
2 teaspoons minced garlic
1 onion (about 5 oz/150 g), chopped
2 cups (200 g) cauliflower florets
1 teaspoon Asian red chili powder or
    cayenne pepper
1 teaspoon Café Spice Garam Masala
    (page 22)
½ teaspoon ground coriander
½ teaspoon ground cumin
Salt, to taste
Juice of 1 lime
4 tablespoons chopped coriander leaves
    (cilantro)
Butter or ghee, for brushing the rolls
8 slider buns or mini potato rolls

Combine the potatoes with enough cold water to cover, in a large saucepan. Bring it to a boil over high heat and cook, uncovered, until tender, about 15–20 minutes. Drain well and set aside to cool. Peel the potatoes, return them to the pan and mash. Set aside.

Make a small cross with a knife on the top of the tomatoes. In a large saucepan, boil enough water to cover the tomatoes. Add the tomatoes to the boiling water and bring it to a boil, about 1–2 minutes and turn off the heat. Allow to stand for about 5 minutes. Drain and allow to cool slightly, then peel off the skins. Mash the pulp and set aside.

If using fresh peas, cook them in a small saucepan with enough boiling water for 5–7 minutes or until soft.

Heat a large, nonstick griddle pan or a skillet over medium heat and add the butter or ghee. Add the minced garlic and onion and cook, stirring often, until translucent for about 3–4 minutes. Turn the heat to high and add the tomato pulp, mashed potatoes, green peas, and cauliflower florets. Add the ground spices and salt and continue to stir and mash with a spatula or a potato masher until well combined. Cook for about 5 minutes. It is your choice how mashed you want the vegetables

to be. Fold in the lime juice and coriander leaves.

Prepare the buns or rolls before serving. Heat a flat griddle over medium heat. Melt the butter or ghee until the pan is coated. Place the buns or rolls and toast them until slightly brown on all sides, about 2–3 minutes.

Serve the buns or rolls hot alongside the mashed vegetables.

Goan Fish Cakes Macchi Tikki

The rice flour in this recipe is added mostly as a binder, as fish is very flaky. Canned or fresh lump crabmeat works great with this recipe. The beauty of this dish is that it can be made in advance and kept refrigerated or frozen, and fried as needed—so that unannounced guests can get a treat too! You can make a healthier version by omitting the potato and by pan-frying the cakes. This can certainly be an appetizer, but if serving as part of a meal, make sure there are other wet courses like a dal or a soup that complement it.

Serves 4
Prep time: **20 minutes**
Cook time: **20 minutes**

1 lb/500 g fish fillet (cod, halibut, or bass)
2 cups (500 ml) fish stock or water, to poach
1 potato, about 8 oz (250 g) boiled, peeled and grated
1 red onion (about 4 oz/125 g), minced
1 fresh green chili pepper, minced
1 teaspoon minced ginger
1 teaspoon toasted cumin seeds, coarsely ground
2 tablespoons chopped coriander leaves (cilantro)
2 tablespoons rice flour
Salt, to taste
Freshly ground black pepper, to taste
1 egg, separated
Oil, to deep-fry

In a medium saucepan over medium heat, add the fish with the fish stock or water and poach gently for about 10 minutes until just tender. Drain, reserving ¼ cup (65 ml) of the stock. Transfer the fish to a large mixing bowl. Flake the fish using a fork, removing any small residual bones.

Add the grated potato, onion, chili, ginger, cumin seeds, and chopped coriander into a bowl and mix well. Sprinkle in the flour and stir to mix. Moisten with the reserved fish stock if needed and season with salt and pepper to taste. Add the egg yolk and mix well to combine. Divide the mixture into 16 pieces and shape into croquettes or rolls.

Heat 2 inches (5 cm) of oil in a kadhai, small wok, or large saucepan over medium heat to 325°F (160°C) on a deep-fry or candy thermometer. To gauge the temperature of the oil without a thermometer, drop a piece of bread about 1-in (2.5-cm) square into the oil, turning the piece of bread often as the oil heats up. When the oil reaches 325°F (160°C), the bread will begin to brown quickly and turn golden brown all over—like a crouton—in about 40 seconds.

Beat the egg white. Dip the fish rolls into the egg white, then deep-fry for 2–3 minutes or until golden. Drain on paper towels. Serve hot.

Vegetable Wrap Kati Roll

The "*kati* roll," as it is called in the eastern city of Kolkata in India, or the "Frankie," as the locals of Mumbai call it, is an extremely popular and quick "short eat." In fact, even in certain American cities, you can find small eateries and restaurants selling the kati roll—otherwise known as the "Indian burrito." Given below is my version of a healthy, Indo-American kati roll. Best served with Mint Chutney (page 27) and a side salad of crisp greens.

Serves 4
Prep time: 20 minutes
Cook time: 15 minutes

4 tablespoons oil
1 teaspoon cumin seeds
1 teaspoon minced fresh ginger
1 fresh green chili pepper, chopped
1 red onion (about 4 oz/125 g), thinly sliced
1 carrot, peeled and cut into thin strips
1 small red pepper, cut into thin strips
¼ lb (125 g) white cabbage, cut into thin
    strips
1 portabella mushroom (about 5 oz/150 g)
    stem removed and thinly sliced
1 teaspoon Asian red chili powder or
    cayenne pepper
1 teaspoon ground turmeric
1 teaspoon ground coriander
1 teaspoon Café Spice Garam Masala
    (page 22)
Salt, to taste
4 oz (125 g) Paneer Cheese (page 76), cut
    into strips (optional)
Juice of ½ lime
4 tablespoons chopped coriander leaves
    (cilantro)

4 large *chapati* (page 122) or whole wheat
    tortilla wraps, about 12 in (30 cm)

Heat the oil over medium heat in a large nonstick skillet. Add the cumin seeds and let them crackle, and then add the ginger, green chili, and onion. Sauté gently until the onion is softened and translucent, about 2–3 minutes. Add the carrot, red pepper, cabbage, and mushrooms and sauté for a minute. Add the ground spices and salt and cook for 2–3 minutes until the vegetables soften slightly. Add the paneer strips (if using) and toss to mix. Remove from the heat and allow to cool. Add the lemon juice and chopped coriander leaves and set aside.

To assemble, lay the flat breads on a clean surface, spoon the filling onto the center of the wrap. Fold the ends over and enclose and fold over the sides. Roll up, holding the ends, to enclose the filling. Serve the wraps warm or cold.

Stuffed Lamb Fritters Shami Kebab

This is one of Sushil's favorite kebabs, and we often make them for cocktail parties. The preparation is a little time consuming, but they're rather simple to make. The combination of mint leaves and the sharpness of the red onions that you discover when you bite into these fritters will definitely leave you wanting more. This dish is great as a party starter or a part of a weekend dinner at home.

Serves 4
Prep time: 20 minutes, plus 30 minutes for cooling
Cook time: 1 hour

1 lb (500 g) ground lamb
¾ cup (185 ml) water
4 tablespoons split yellow peas (chana dal), rinsed
1 tablespoon minced garlic
1 teaspoon cumin seeds
5 green cardamom pods
2 cloves
1 cinnamon stick, 1-in (2.5-cm)
2 fresh green chili peppers, chopped
2 tablespoons oil, plus more for deep-frying
2 tablespoons lemon juice
1 teaspoon Asian red chili powder or cayenne pepper
Salt, to taste
1 red onion (about 4 oz/125 g), minced
1 tablespoon chopped mint leaves
2 boiled egg whites, chopped

In a large, heavy-bottomed saucepan over medium heat, add the ground lamb, water, split peas, garlic, cumin seeds, cardamom pods, cloves, cinnamon, and chili peppers and bring to a boil. Reduce the heat to medium and cook until the water is absorbed and the meat is completely dry, about 30–40 minutes. Add the oil and cook, stirring for another 2–3 minutes. Remove from the heat and set aside to cool completely, about 30–45 minutes.

Transfer the lamb mixture (make sure you remove the cinnamon stick) into a blender or a food processor. Add the lemon juice, chili powder, and salt and process to a fine paste. Transfer this mixture to a bowl, divide into 8 equal portions, and roll each into a ball. Refrigerate for 30 minutes to an hour. Meanwhile, mix the chopped red onion, egg whites, and mint in a small bowl and set aside.

Dip your hands in some water and with wet hands flatten each lamb ball. Then add about ¼ teaspoon of the onion-mint mixture into the center, seal, and flatten again into a round patty. Repeat this process to stuff all 8 patties.

Meanwhile, heat 2 inches (5 cm) of oil in a kadhai, small wok or large saucepan over medium heat to 325°F (160°C) on a deep-fry or candy thermometer. To gauge the temperature of the oil without a thermometer, drop a piece of bread about 1-in (2.5-cm) square into the oil, turning the piece of bread often as the oil heats up. When the oil reaches 325°F (160°C), the bread will begin to brown quickly and turn golden brown all over—like a crouton—in about 40 seconds. Working in small batches, deep-fry the lamb patties, turning frequently for 2–3 minutes until crisp and golden. Drain on paper towels. Serve hot. Alternately the patties can be shallow fried, cooking on both sides for about 2–3 minutes.

Crab and Coconut Salad

Although very simple to make, this dish might not end up being your everyday salad, since fresh crabmeat is a novelty and an expensive ingredient in most American groceries. Either lump crabmeat or canned crabmeat can be used for this recipe. The tempering using typical south Indian-style ingredients makes the taste of this salad unique. Coconut gives it a very nice texture and flavor. In case you have leftovers (which I seriously doubt!), you can use them in a wrap, with some lettuce and tomatoes or pocket them in pita bread for a quick working lunch.

Serves **3**
Prep time: **10 minutes**
Cook time: **5 minutes**

3 tablespoons oil
2 teaspoons mustard seeds
5 fresh curry leaves, minced
1 teaspoon minced fresh peeled ginger
1 fresh green chili pepper, seeds removed, and minced
1 small red onion (about 4 oz/125 g), sliced
½ teaspoon ground turmeric
½ teaspoon ground cumin
Salt, to taste
3 cups (300 g) crabmeat, freshly prepared or canned
3 tablespoons coconut milk
1 tablespoon grated fresh coconut
1 tablespoon chopped coriander leaves (cilantro)

Heat the oil in a nonstick pan over medium heat, add the mustard seeds, and sauté until they splutter. Add the curry leaves, ginger, and green chili pepper and cook, stirring for another minute. Add the sliced onions and sauté until softened and translucent, about 2 minutes. Add the turmeric, cumin, salt, and crabmeat, stir for a few seconds. Sauté for 2 minutes, then stir in the coconut milk, grated coconut, and chopped coriander. Remove from the heat and set aside to cool. Serve the salad cold, with Spiced Pear Chutney (page 26) and some salad greens.

Shrimp Stuffed Pappadum   Jhinja Bharwan Papad

Pappadums, sometimes called *papads*, are dried disks of dough made from legume flours. They are often flavored with chili pepper, black pepper, garlic, and cumin seeds. Some will be brittle and so thin that they're almost translucent, while others will be relatively thick and made perhaps from a different kind of legume. Pappadums are a great way to bring additional flavor and texture to an Indian meal. Sometimes they are just the added touch that completes a meal.

There are several different ways to cook the pappadums. A common way is to deep-fry them by sliding them one at a time into a skillet filled with hot oil. They will instantly start to expand and change color. With a pair of metal tongs, try to hold each one under the surface of the oil until the whole disk has cooked, a process that should take no more than 5–7 seconds. Remove from the fryer, drain the excess oil, and stack them to cool and become crisp. Another cooking method is to hold each pappadum over the flame of a gas burner or a grill for about 1 minute, quickly exposing all sides and edges to the heat. They crinkle up into beautiful shapes almost at once and become very crisp as they cool. But while they are still warm, they can be shaped into pockets, rolls, or other desired shapes. Cooked pappadums can be stuffed or topped with toasted coconut, chopped herbs, spice mixtures, minced meats, and nuts. Here is a quick recipe for stuffed pappadums. I describe filling them with fresh shrimps, but you can be creative and use any stuffing you like. Spiced mashed potatoes, minced meat, or mixed vegetables will work well. Serve this with a dipping sauce or chutney. Try the Spiced Pear Chutney (page 26) as it goes with it very well.

Serves 4
Prep time: **15 minutes**
Cook time: **15 minutes**

1 tablespoon oil
1 large onion (about 8 oz/250 g), minced
1 teaspoon minced garlic
1 teaspoon minced fresh ginger
1 teaspoon freshly ground black pepper
¼ teaspoon ground coriander
½ teaspoon ground turmeric
½ lb (250 g) fresh, medium-size shrimp (about
    15–18), peeled, deveined, and chopped
1 small potato, about 5 oz (150 g) boiled, peeled
    and chopped
1 teaspoon lemon juice
Salt, to taste
2 tablespoons chopped coriander leaves (cilantro)
8 plain or spicy *papads* (uncooked pappadums)
1 tablespoon all-purpose flour
Oil, to deep-fry

To make the stuffing, heat the oil in a large nonstick skillet over medium heat. Add the onion, garlic, ginger, and black pepper and sauté until the onion is soft and translucent, about 5 minutes.

Add the ground coriander, turmeric, and chopped shrimp. Sauté for 3–4 minutes and then add the cooked potatoes, lemon juice, and salt. Sprinkle with the chopped coriander leaves. Mix well and set aside to cool.

Meanwhile, soak the papad disks in warm water for 5–8 minutes to soften and then drain. In a small bowl, mix the flour with a few drops of water to form a paste. This will act as glue. Spoon the shrimp mixture on to one side of the papads, then roll up, folding in the sides and sealing the edges with the flour paste, to form a roll.

Heat 2 inches (5 cm) of oil in a *kadhai*, small wok, or large saucepan over medium heat to 325°F (160°C) on a deep-fry or candy thermometer. To gauge the temperature of the oil without a thermometer, drop a piece of bread about 1-in (2.5-cm) square into the oil, turning the piece of bread often as the oil heats up. When the oil reaches 325°F (160°C), the bread will begin to brown quickly and turn golden brown all over—like a crouton—in about 40 seconds. Deep-fry the stuffed papads in batches, turning frequently for 2–3 minutes until crisp and golden. Drain on paper towels. Serve hot.

Chopped Vegetable Salad   Khachumbar Salaad

In India, or in Indian cuisine, salads are usually served as a relish and an accompaniment rather than in the traditional way a Western meal would feature a salad. However, I have made this salad with the thought in mind that Americans usually treat salad as a proper course by itself. Add as many vegetables as you want—this can be made into a whole meal. Or, if you intend to serve it as part of a meal, serve small portions, as this salad can be quite filling. I have used unconventional greens—baby spinach instead of lettuce. The salad also has the goodness of honey, as an alternative sweetening agent.

Serves 4
Prep time: 20 minutes

2 cucumbers (about 1 lb/500 g), peeled, cut in half lengthwise and diced
1 carrot, peeled and diced
1 red onion (about 5 oz/150 g) diced
1 cup (150 g) cherry tomatoes, halved
¼ cup (25 gm) fresh or frozen sweet corn kernels
2 cups (100 g) packed fresh baby spinach leaves, washed

LEMON HONEY DRESSING
3 tablespoons freshly squeezed lemon juice
2 teaspoons honey
3 tablespoons extra-virgin olive oil
Salt, to taste
½ teaspoon dried red pepper flakes
1 tablespoon minced fresh mint leaves
2 teaspoons cumin seeds, toasted and coarsely ground

Whisk together the ingredients for the Lemon Honey Dressing in a small bowl until well blended. Set aside.
Mix together the cucumbers, carrot, onion, tomatoes, corn, and baby spinach in a large mixing bowl.
Pour on the Lemon Honey Dressing and toss gently. Transfer to a serving bowl and serve chilled.

Sweet Potato and Sprout Salad

The idea for this recipe struck me once when I had a lot of roasted sweet potatoes left over from a family Thanksgiving dinner. I conveniently used the surplus to make a salad the next day. Very soon, this became a habit! I use *chaat* masala in this salad to bring out the flavors of the cooked sweet potato. You can also use dried raw mango powder and black or sea salt to do the same and bring out the uniqueness of Indian flavor. During winter in India, sweet potato *chaat* is sold by street-side vendors and is a very popular evening snack.

Serves 4
Prep time: **10 minutes**
Cook time: **30 minutes**

2 large (about 1 lb/500 g) sweet potatoes
3 tablespoons oil
1 cup (100 g) bean sprouts
1 apple, peeled, cored, and diced
2 cups (125 g) diced romaine or iceberg lettuce

LEMON MINT DRESSING
3 tablespoons freshly squeezed lemon juice
1 teaspoons honey
3 tablespoons extra-virgin olive oil
1 tablespoon Mint Chutney (page 27)
2 tablespoons minced coriander leaves (cilantro)
2 teaspoons Chaat Masala (page 22, optional)

Preheat the oven to 400ºF (200ºC). Apply one tablespoon of oil to the sweet potatoes. Place them on a baking sheet and bake for 20–30 minutes until soft. Peel and dice. Set aside.
While the potatoes are cooking, whisk together the ingredients for the Lemon Mint Dressing in a small bowl until well blended. Set aside.
Heat the remaining oil in a small nonstick pan over medium-high heat and fry the sweet potatoes until light golden brown. Set aside in a large mixing bowl. (Frying is optional, as you can use baked sweet potato as is.) To serve, toss the sweet potatoes with the bean sprouts, apples, lettuce and Lemon Mint Dressing. Transfer to a serving bowl and serve chilled.

Chickpea, Mango and Watercress Salad

This recipe contains shredded raw mango. If you find it is a challenge to find fresh mangoes, you can easily substitute any other crunchy vegetable like radish or jicama. Also, this recipe uses olive oil, which is not a very traditional ingredient in Indian cuisine. This salad has partially been inspired by the very popular Thai raw mango and papaya salad, but selected Indian spices and grains add an interesting twist. The bitterness of watercress works well to balance the sourness of the mangoes.

Serves 4
Prep time: **20 minutes**
Cook time:**10 minutes**

1 tablespoon extra-virgin olive oil
1 teaspoon mustard seeds
2 teaspoons split black gram (urad dal)
5–6 fresh curry leaves, minced
1 fresh green chili pepper, minced
½ teaspoon red chili flakes
1 can chickpeas 15½-oz (439-g), drained and rinsed well
1 teaspoon salt
3 tablespoons shredded coconut, fresh or frozen
1 green mango (about 8 oz/250 g) peeled and cut into thin
   strips
Watercress
1 apple, cored and cut into thin strips (optional)
Grated zest and juice of 1 lemon

Heat the oil in a small skillet over medium heat. Add the
   mustard seeds and black gram and sauté for 30 seconds
   until the mixture splutters. Then add the curry leaves, green
   chili, and red chili flakes and sauté for another minute. Add
   the cooked chickpeas and salt and sauté for another minute
   or 2 and then remove from the heat.
Let it cool for 5–10 minutes. Add the coconut, mango,
   watercress, apple (if using), and lemon zest and juice. Toss
   to mix all the salad ingredients together and check the
   seasoning.

Potato and Pea Samosas Aloo Aur Matar Samosae

At Café Spice we make more than 10,000 handmade samosas a day! The samosa is a quintessential Indian snack and is probably the most common snack served when you have unexpected visitors. Every neighborhood in India has at least one vendor selling these delicious triangular fritters. Although the standard stuffing for samosas is potato, you can be very innovative and use ingredients like leftover lentils, vegetables, or even minced meat for the filling. The preparation is simple—if you can consistently form triangle shapes, you can make samosas. Various machines and equipment have been tried to form the perfect swollen triangle from the dough, but to date, the best samosas are still made by hand. At the Café Spice kitchen, we have a dedicated samosa room and employ skilled "samosa girls" who have mastered the art of consistently churning out these perfect triangle shapes.

Serves 4
Prep time: 30 minutes
Cook time: 15 minutes

SAMOSA PASTRY

2 cups (240 g) all-purpose flour
½ teaspoon salt
¼ teaspoon nigella seeds (optional)
4 tablespoons plus 1 teaspoon oil
4 tablespoons water, plus more if needed

POTATO AND PEAS FILLING

4 tablespoons oil
1 teaspoon mustard seeds
1 onion (about 5 oz/150 g), diced
1 teaspoon ground coriander
1 teaspoon Asian red chili powder or cayenne pepper
1 teaspoon salt
½ teaspoon ground turmeric
2 potatoes (about 1¼ lbs/600 g), peeled and diced
1 cup (130 g) green peas, fresh or frozen (shelled from 1 lb/500 g fresh pea pods)

To make the Samosa Pastry: Sift the flour and salt into a bowl. Add the nigella seeds (if using) and 4 tablespoons of oil and rub the ingredients in with your fingers until the mixture resembles coarse breadcrumbs. Slowly add about 4 tablespoons water and form the dough into a stiff ball, adding more water if needed.

Knead the dough on a floured surface for about 5–7 minutes, until smooth, and make a ball. Rub the remaining 1 teaspoon of oil on the surface of the dough ball and set it aside for at least 30 minutes, making sure it is tightly wrapped with plastic wrap. While the Samosa Pastry is resting, make the samosa filling.

To make the Potato and Peas Filling: Heat the oil in a skillet over medium heat. Add the mustard seeds, and when they start to pop, add the onion and fry until soft. Add the ground coriander, Asian red chili powder or cayenne pepper, salt, and ground turmeric and cook, stirring constantly, for about 30 seconds. Add the potatoes and green peas. Cover and cook for 15 minutes, stirring frequently, until the potatoes are cooked. Remove from the heat and set aside.

When you are ready to fill the samosas, divide the Samosa Pastry into 8 balls. It is important to work with one ball of dough at time and to keep the other dough balls covered to prevent drying. Take a ball and roll it out into a 7-in (18-cm) circle. Cut it in half with a sharp knife. Working with one of the half-circles, with the straight edge positioned at the top, fold one of the sides inward to the center. With your finger, rub a little water on the top of folded edge. Now take the other side and fold it inward, overlapping the moistened dough edge to form a cone. Press the two edges together. Fill the cone with about 2 tablespoons of the filling of your choice. Do not over fill the samosa. It is very important that there is at least a ¼-in (6-mm)-wide border of dough along the top to make sure the filling does not come out while frying. With your finger, rub a little water along the inside edge of the dough at the top of the cone. Close the top of the cone by firmly pressing the open edges together. Press the top seam down with back side of the fork, or flute it with your fingers. Fill the rest of the samosas.

Heat 2 inches (5 cm) of oil in a kadhai, small wok, or large saucepan over medium heat to 325°F (160°C) on a deep-fry or candy thermometer. To gauge the temperature of the oil without a thermometer, drop a piece of bread about 1-in (2.5-cm) square into the oil, turning the piece of bread often as the oil heats up. When the oil reaches 325°F (160°C), the bread will begin to brown quickly and turn golden brown all over—like a crouton—in about 40 seconds. Deep-fry the samosa in batches, turning frequently, until golden brown and crisp. Remove them with a slotted spoon and drain on paper towels. Serve hot or at room temperature.

Chapter 4 SOUPS AND DALS

As far as Indian soups go, the possibilities are endless. They can be eaten as a part of the meal or made into a bigger portion that's good for a full meal. Many soups such as tomato and sweet corn have taken the front page in our Indian restaurant menus and are the perfect start your meal.

Indian-flavored soups receive a different treatment during preparation than their Western counterparts. The delicate use of spices like cumin seeds with a dash of green chili, in combination with fresh herbs, lentils, and vegetables imparts special aromas to these soups and makes them a perfect match for Indian fare. Some parts of India have extreme winter conditions, and some soups—especially the ones that contain spices like ginger, cinnamon, and peppercorn—are meant to combat the chill. Most of these soups would also make a delicious and substantial lunch, perhaps served with some Indian bread such as Naan Bread (page 121), or as an imaginative start to a dinner party. These soups are easy to prepare and most can be made ahead of time and then reheated just before serving. You can use a blender or a food processor for preparing most of these soups and make them thick or thin in consistency as you like. Indian soups are almost never thickened with starch, unlike Western soups.

Dal or lentils are also an integral part of Indian cuisine. Dal is often eaten with rice in the southern part of India, as well as with Indian breads in the north. Dal has an exceptional nutritional profile. It provides an excellent source of protein, particularly for those eating vegetarian diets or diets that do not contain much meat. Dal is also high in carbohydrates while being virtually fat free. Most dal recipes are quite simple to prepare. The standard preparation begins with boiling a variety of dal (or a mix) in water with some turmeric, salt to taste, and then adding a fried garnish at the end of the cooking process. In some recipes, tomatoes, tamarind, unripe mango, or other ingredients are added while cooking the dal, often to impart a sour flavor. Sometimes red kidney beans, chickpeas and other heavy legumes are used to make preparations that are a cross between a dal and gravy. *Rajmah* (Red Kidney Bean Dal, page 51) is usually served with rice. Although the recipes for dal used in this book are all vegetarian, feel free to add meat in some of the preparations. For example, you could use minced chicken, turkey, or pork in some of the recipes, per your preference, and make them into a wholesome dinner bowl!

Green Pea Soup **Matar Shorba**

For a comforting starter or simple meal on a cold day, try a bowl of warm pea soup. This soup can provide several benefits as part of an overall balanced diet. It is high in fiber, a great source of essential minerals and vitamins, and also has some contribution to weight loss, if some study reports are to be believed. The soup tastes great when made with fresh green peas that are in season, but when made with frozen peas, it tastes just as delicious.

Serves 4
Prep time: **15 minutes**
Cook time: **30 minutes**

2 tablespoons butter
2 cups (200 g) fresh green peas shelled
2 cups (100 g) packed fresh spinach leaves, washed and chopped
or ¾ cup (150 g) frozen chopped spinach, thawed
1 tablespoon chopped fresh mint leaves
2½ cups (625 ml) water or vegetable stock
1 cup (250 ml) cream
Salt, to taste
Freshly ground black pepper, to taste
¼ teaspoon sugar
¼ teaspoon nutmeg powder
¼ teaspoon Café Spice Garam Masala (page 22)
Juice of ½ lime

Melt 1 teaspoon of the butter in a large saucepan over medium heat add the green peas, spinach, and mint and cook for 30 seconds. Add the water or vegetable stock and bring it to a boil. Lower the heat and simmer covered for 25–30 minutes. Remove from the heat and let it cool. Using a table top or a hand blender, purée the mixture until very smooth. Pass it through a strainer for a smooth texture.

Melt the remaining butter in a large saucepot over medium heat, add the strained pea soup, cream, salt, black pepper, sugar, nutmeg, and Garam Masala. Bring to a boil, simmer for 2 minutes, and then remove from the heat. Add the lime juice before serving. Serve hot.

Red Kidney Bean Dal
Rajmah

This dish is extremely popular, not just in northern India, but elsewhere as well. It is a very popular weekend brunch dish, often served with plain rice. The consistency of this dish can be thicker, for scooping with roti bread or even whole grain tortillas or made thinner to serve over rice and eaten like a stew. Serve Rajmah with Simple Rice Pilaf (page 120), Chopped Vegetable Salad (page 43), and your favorite pickle.

Serves 4

Prep time: 15 minutes plus 8 hours soaking time if using dried kidney beans

Cook time: 55 minutes (1 hour 20 minutes if using dried kidney beans)

2 cups (350 g), dried red kidney beans, soaked overnight and drained, or two 15½-oz (439-g) cans kidney beans, rinsed and drained

½ cup (100 g), split black gram (urad dal), soaked overnight and drained

10 cups (2.5 liters) water plus ½ tablespoon salt for cooking the dried beans

½ cup (125 ml) oil

1 tablespoon cumin seeds

1 teaspoon fennel seeds

1 large onion (about 8 oz/250 g), minced

4 tablespoons Ginger-Garlic Paste (page 22)

3 fresh green chili peppers, minced

3 large tomatoes (about 1½ lbs/750 g), minced

3 teaspoons ground coriander

2 teaspoons Asian red chili powder or cayenne pepper

Salt, to taste

2 teaspoons Café Spice Garam Masala (page 22)

4 tablespoons chopped fresh coriander leaves (cilantro)

2 tablespoons butter (optional)

If using dried kidney beans, bring the soaked and drained beans, split black gram, water, and salt to a boil in a large saucepan. Reduce the heat to low, cover, and simmer until the beans are tender, about 45–50 minutes. Drain the beans, but reserve the cooking liquid. Set aside.

Heat the oil in a large, heavy-bottomed skillet or saucepan over medium heat. Add the cumin seeds and fennel seeds. Let them sizzle for 10 seconds. Add the onion and cook, stirring frequently, until soft and starting to brown, about 5 minutes. Add the Ginger-Garlic Paste and fry for 1–2 minutes until soft. Add the green chili peppers, tomatoes, ground coriander, Asian red chili powder or cayenne pepper, salt, and 1 cup (250 ml) of the reserved bean-soaking liquid or water. Cover and cook over low heat until the masala is cooked, about 5 minutes.

Add the cooked or canned red kidney beans to the tomato gravy and simmer, adding more of the bean-soaking liquid or water as needed, about 5–10 minutes. Stir in the Café Spice Garam Masala, fresh coriander leaves, and butter (if using). Serve hot.

Lentil and Spinach Soup Dal Palak

You can have this soup any time of the year, but it is especially great when the weather is cold! Serve it with Naan Bread (page 121), bread sticks, crusty bread, or have it just by itself. This soup has a refreshing, rustic simplicity that makes it feel like a safe haven amidst culinary fussiness. It is revitalizing and nourishing—a wonderful one-bowl meal to savor. Soaking the lentils for 4–8 hours will help them cook faster, but it's not essential. If you do soak them, use a smaller quantity of water during cooking, as they will have already absorbed liquid while soaking. This soup keeps well in the fridge for up to a week; add fresh spinach if you want it to stay green.

Serves 4
Prep time: 15 minutes
Cook time: 30 minutes

1 tablespoon oil
1 teaspoon cumin seeds
1 red onion (about 5 oz/150 g), chopped
2 large cloves garlic, crushed
1 teaspoon ginger powder
½ teaspoon Café Spice Garam Masala (page 22)
¼ teaspoon ground turmeric
1 small tomato (about 3 oz/85 g), chopped
1 cup (175 g) yellow lentils, rinsed and drained
2 cups (500 ml) water
3 cups (150 g) packed fresh spinach leaves, washed and chopped, or
    1 cup (200 g) frozen chopped spinach, thawed
½ cup (125 ml) coconut milk
Salt, to taste
2 tablespoons chopped fresh coriander leaves (cilantro)

Heat the oil in a large saucepan over medium heat. Add the cumin seeds— they should sizzle on contact with the hot oil. Add the onion, garlic, ginger powder, Café Spice Garam Masala, and turmeric and cook, stirring constantly, until the spices are fragrant, about 1 minute. Add the tomato and cook for another 30 seconds.

Add the lentils and water and bring to a boil over medium-high heat. Reduce the heat to low, cover partially, and simmer until the lentils are tender, about 15–20 minutes. Add more water if you want the dal to be thinner. If you want the soup to be a smooth purée, use a hand blender to purée the mixture now.

Stir in the spinach, coconut milk, and salt. Cover and simmer until the spinach is cooked, about 3 more minutes. Serve hot, garnished with the fresh coriander leaves.

Cauliflower and Curry Soup
Gobhi Shorba

Cauliflower is easy to find and quite inexpensive. If you find yourself waiting for true spring produce (peas, favas, and asparagus), this is a good recipe to tide you over. One nice thing is that it takes very little time to pull together. You simply cook down the onions and garlic with the cauliflower, broth, and warm spices and prepare your favorite toppings (I like roasted potatoes, toasty cashews, and spicy red chili flakes—all with a dash of olive oil). Try it with coconut milk instead of heavy cream. Use skim milk for a lighter soup or skip dairy products completely for a vegan option.

Serves 4
Prep time: **15 minutes**
Cook time: **30 minutes**

1 teaspoon black peppercorns
4 whole cloves
5 green cardamom pods, crushed
1 stick cinnamon, ½-in (1.25-cm)
1 tablespoon fennel seeds
2 tablespoons butter
1 small onion (about 4 oz/125 g), chopped
4 large cloves garlic, minced
1 piece fresh ginger, 1-in (2.5-cm), peeled and chopped
6 cups (600 g) cauliflower florets (from 2½ lbs/1 kg cauliflower)
1 teaspoon Café Spice Garam Masala (page 22)
Salt, to taste
7 cups (1.75 liters) vegetable stock or water
1 cup (250 ml) heavy cream

Place the peppercorns, cloves, cardamom, cinnamon, and fennel seeds in a small piece of cheesecloth and tie the cloth closed with a knot. Melt the butter in a medium saucepan over medium heat. Add the onion, garlic, ginger, cauliflower florets, Café Spice Garam Masala, and salt. Cook, stirring constantly, for 1 minute. Add the vegetable stock or water and the spice pouch. Simmer for 20–25 minutes or until the cauliflower is tender. Remove from the heat and discard the bag of spices. Let the soup cool slightly.

Purée the cooled soup in a food processor or blender until smooth. Force the soup through a strainer into a clean saucepan. Add the heavy cream and bring the soup to a simmer. Ladle into soup bowls and serve hot.

Chickpea Curry with Sweet Potato Shakkar Kandi Chana Masala

This is a version of *chana masala*, a chickpea dish that is unquestionably one of the most popular vegetable curry dishes in northern India, and the most versatile. It is served as a one-dish meal at all times of day or as a snack. Its blend of fragrant spices is warming and healthy. Serve with a dollop of natural yogurt and a sprig of coriander. I use ghee in this recipe, but for a healthier version, use vegetable oil. Try serving this with Fried Puffed Bread (page 125) or Potato and Pea Samosas (page 46).

Serves 4
Prep time: **15 minutes plus 8 hours soaking time if using dried chickpeas**
Cook time: **30 minutes (1 hour 15 minutes if using dried chickpeas)**

2 cups (350 g), dried chickpeas, soaked overnight and drained, or three 15½-oz (439-g) cans chickpeas, drained and rinsed well
4 cups (1 liter) water plus ½ teaspoon salt for cooking dried peas
½ cup (125 ml) oil
1 tablespoon plus 1 teaspoon Ginger-Garlic Paste (page 22)
1 tablespoon plus 1 teaspoon coriander seeds, crushed
1 tablespoon plus 1 teaspoon cumin seeds, crushed
2 onions (about ¾ lb/350 g), minced
4 fresh green chili peppers, slit open lengthwise
1 piece fresh ginger, 1-in (2.5-cm), peeled and chopped
½ lb (250 g) sweet potatoes, peeled and cut into 1-in (2.5-cm) dice
2 tomatoes (about ¾ lb/350 g), minced
2 teaspoons salt
2 teaspoons Café Spice Garam Masala (page 22)
1 teaspoon Asian red chili powder or cayenne pepper
1 cup (250 ml) water

3 cups (150 g) packed fresh baby spinach leaves, washed

2 tablespoons freshly squeezed lemon juice

1 teaspoon dried fenugreek leaves (*kasoori methi*) (optional)

4 tablespoons chopped fresh coriander leaves (cilantro)

If using dried chickpeas, bring the soaked and drained peas, water, and ½ teaspoon of salt to a boil in a large saucepan over high heat. Reduce the heat to low and simmer, covered, until the peas are tender, about 45 minutes. Drain the peas, rinse with cold water, and drain again. Set aside.

Heat the oil in a medium saucepan over medium heat. Add the Ginger-Garlic Paste and fry for about 30 seconds, stirring constantly. Add the crushed coriander and cumin seeds and fry for 15–20 seconds, stirring constantly, until fragrant.

Add the onions, green chili peppers, and ginger and cook over medium heat, stirring often, until the onions are uniformly dark brown in color, about 10–12 minutes. Add the diced sweet potatoes and cook, stirring constantly, making sure the onions do not stick to the pan. Add a little water if necessary. Add the tomatoes, salt, Café Spice Garam Masala, and Asian red chili powder or cayenne pepper and cook, stirring constantly, for about 30 seconds. Add the 1 cup (250 ml) of water, chickpeas, and spinach and bring to a simmer. Cook gently, partially covered, for 15 minutes, stirring occasionally. Stir in the lemon juice, fenugreek, and fresh coriander leaves. Taste for seasoning and add more salt if needed. Serve hot.

South Indian Lentils and Vegetables   Sambhar

Use any available, seasonal vegetables to make this dish. There is an alternate, shorter method using store-bought sambar powder, which is readily available in ethnic stores (my favorite brand is MTR). If you are using store-bought powder, add it along with the lentils and water and bring it to a boil. Just be sure to read the instructions on the packet for the ratio of powder to the broth, as each brand has slightly different ingredients. I like to add a pinch of asafetida to this recipe, as this is how my mother made it at home, and it is a common ingredient in southern Indian cooking. Asafetida's mild garlicky flavor adds a nice dimension to the soup, plus it is said to have beneficial digestive properties. This soup is traditionally served with *dosai* (page 124) as part of the main meal rather than as a first course.

Serves 4
Prep time: **15 minutes**
Cook time: **45 minutes**

8 dried red chili peppers
15–20 curry leaves
2 teaspoons coriander seeds
1 tablespoon split yellow peas (chana dal)
2 teaspoons fenugreek seeds
¾ cup (200 g) split pigeon pea lentils (toor dal)
Salt, to taste
7 cups (1.75 liters) water
2 tablespoons vegetable oil
1 teaspoon mustard seeds
1 teaspoon fennel seeds
½ teaspoon cumin seeds
2 baby eggplants (Asian, about 8 oz/250 g) trimmed and cut into ¾-in (2-cm) pieces
1 carrot, peeled and diced (about ¾ cup/112 g)
1 small potato, peeled and diced (about ¾ cup/130 g)
¼ lb (125 g) fresh green beans, trimmed and cut into 1-in (2.5-cm) lengths
1 cup (250 ml) water
1 tablespoon tamarind paste
4 tablespoons chopped fresh coriander leaves

Heat a cast iron pan over medium heat. Add 4 of the dried red chili peppers, half the curry leaves, coriander seeds, split yellow peas, and fenugreek seeds. Carefully roast the spices, stirring constantly, until toasted and fragrant, about 2–3 minutes. Remove the pan from the heat and allow to cool completely. Use a spice grinder or mortar and pestle to grind the spices into a powder. Pour the powder into a small bowl and add enough water, about 3–4 tablespoons, to form a thick paste. This can be made ahead of time and stored in the refrigerator for up to 1 week.

Place the split pigeon pea lentils, salt, and remaining curry leaves in a medium saucepan and cover with the water. Bring to a boil over high heat. Once boiling, reduce the heat to low and simmer, covered, until the lentils become soft and mushy. Skim off any scum that rises to the surface during the process. Set aside.

Heat the oil in a large saucepan over medium heat and add the mustard seeds, fennel seeds, cumin seeds, and the remaining dried red chili peppers. Stir in the vegetables and cook, stirring constantly, for a minute. Add the water, cover, and boil until the vegetables are tender, about 10 minutes.

Add the cooked lentils and tamarind paste and bring to a boil. Adjust the water if needed. Stir in the fresh coriander leaves and serve hot.

Buttery Black Lentils Dal Makhni

Traditionally, in restaurants, this lentil dal is simmered overnight on a tandoor oven, which enhances the flavors of the dish. I find that soaking the lentils a little longer than usual does the same. I usually soak them in the evening when I need to make this dish for the next day's lunch. Otherwise you can use a slow cooker if you have one. A low-calorie version is very easy. Replace the cream with 2% milk. Cooking it for a long time makes it rich tasting and creamy even without the cream. Try it; you won't miss the high-calorie version. This recipe requires slow cooking for the best result. It reminds me of my days at Bukhara restaurant, one of the top restaurants of the world, where this dish is known to be the best. I was an intern there, and my job was to stir a big pot of the dal to prevent it from sticking. But I will never forget the compliments on this dish from the guests to the kitchen.

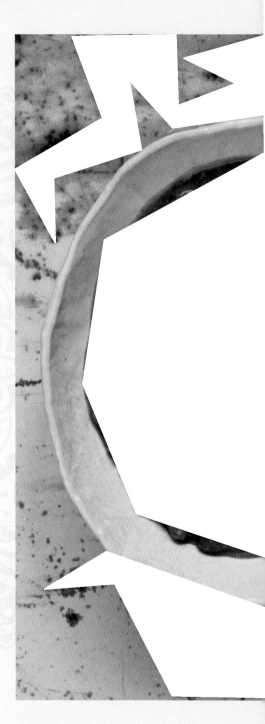

Serves 4
Prep time: 15 minutes, plus 8 hours for soaking
Cook time: 1 hour 30 minutes

2 cups (400 g) whole dried black lentils (urad dal), soaked overnight and drained
8–10 cups (2–2.5 liters) water
1 cup (250 g) tomato paste
1 teaspoon Asian red chili powder or cayenne pepper
2 fresh green chili peppers, slit
Salt, to taste
4 tablespoons Ginger-Garlic Paste (page 22)
3 tablespoons butter
1 piece fresh ginger, ½-in (1.25-cm), peeled cut into thin strips
1 red onion (about 5 oz/150 g), chopped
¼ cup (65 ml) cream
1 teaspoon Café Spice Garam Masala (page 22)
Handful of fresh coriander (cilantro) leaves with stems, chopped

Bring the soaked lentils and water to a boil in a large saucepan. Reduce the heat to low, cover, and simmer until the lentils are tender, about 1 hour.

When the lentils are tender, add the tomato paste, chili powder, green chilies, salt, and the Garlic-Ginger Paste to the pan. Stir well and cook for another 30 minutes. Keep an eye on the pan and give it an occasional stir, as the lentils have a tendency to settle and stick on the bottom.

In a separate small saucepan over low heat, add the butter. When hot, add the onions and sliced ginger and cook for about 4–5 minutes, until translucent. Stir into the lentils along with the cream and Garam Masala. Cook for another minute and served garnished with fresh coriander.

Black-Eyed Pea Curry Lobhia Dal

The black-eyed pea is a versatile pulse that beautifully absorbs the spices added to it, making it succulent and tasty. Better known as *lobhia* in other regions of India, this bean is packed with proteins and micronutrients. I prefer the dried beans to the canned ones because you get the best nutrition from them. Black-eyed peas are high in fiber and rich in potassium and iron. They're also a rich source of protein, so it's good to include them in your regular diet if you are following a vegetarian diet. Preparation of this curry is unusually quick. Serve it with Whole Wheat Griddle Bread (page 122) to complement.

Serves 4
Prep time: **15 minutes plus 8 hours soaking time if using dried black-eyed peas**
Cook time: **55 minutes (1 hour 15 minutes if using dried black-eyed peas)**

1 cup (175 g) dried black-eyed peas, soaked overnight and drained, or 1 can black-eyed peas, 15½-oz (439-g), rinsed and drained
4 cups (1 liter) water plus ½ teaspoon salt for cooking dried peas
¼ cup (65 ml) oil
2 teaspoons cumin seeds
1 cinnamon stick, 1-in (2.5-cm)
1 red onion (about 5 oz/150 g), chopped
1 tablespoon minced garlic
1 lb (500 g) tomatoes, blanched, peeled, and chopped (about 2½ cups/500 g)
2 teaspoons ground coriander
1 teaspoon ground cumin
½ teaspoon ground turmeric
¼ teaspoon asafetida (optional)
½ teaspoon paprika
Salt, to taste
3 tablespoons chopped fresh coriander leaves (cilantro)

If using dried black-eyed peas, bring the soaked and drained peas, water, and ½ teaspoon of salt to a boil in a large saucepan over high heat. Cover and simmer over low heat until the peas are tender, about 45 minutes. Drain the peas, rinse with cold water, and drain again. Set aside.

Heat the oil in a large, heavy-bottomed skillet or saucepan over medium heat. Add the cumin seeds and cinnamon stick and let them sizzle for 10 seconds. Add the onion and garlic and cook, stirring frequently, until soft and starting to brown, about 5 minutes. Add the tomatoes, ground coriander, cumin, turmeric, asafetida (if using), paprika, salt, and a little water, if needed. Cover and cook over low heat for 10 minutes, until tender.

Add the cooked or canned black-eyed peas to the tomato mixture and simmer, uncovered, for 10 minutes. Stir in the fresh coriander leaves. Serve hot.

Homestyle Dal with Pumpkin Kaddu Ki Dal

My grandmother was an excellent cook, and this particular recipe was one of her favorites—and mine as well. She traditionally made it using an Indian variety of orange pumpkin, but any kind of pumpkin (especially sugar pumpkins) or a hard squash (such as butternut or acorn) will work well. The result is always a hearty, healthy soup with a lovely edge of sweetness.

Serves 6
Prep time: 15 minutes
Cook time: 45 minutes

2 cups (350 g) dried masoor dal or split lentils of your choice, washed and drained
8 oz (250 g) pumpkin, peeled and diced into ¾-in (2-cm) dice
7 cups (1.75 liters) water
1 teaspoon ground turmeric
1½ teaspoons salt
3 tablespoons oil
2½ teaspoons cumin seeds
2 dried red chili peppers, broken in half
6–8 fresh curry leaves
2 tablespoons chopped garlic
1 tablespoon peeled and minced fresh ginger
2 fresh green chili peppers, minced
1 tomato (about 5 oz/150 g), diced
1 teaspoon Asian red chili powder or cayenne pepper
4 tablespoons minced fresh coriander leaves (cilantro)
Juice of ½ lime

Bring the lentils, pumpkin, and water to a boil in a heavy pot. Remove any surface scum that collects on top. Add the turmeric and salt and reduce the heat to low. Cover, leaving the lid slightly ajar, and simmer gently for 20–30 minutes or until the lentils become soft and mushy and the pumpkin is fully cooked. Stir often to prevent sticking. Set aside.

Heat the oil in a large saucepan over medium heat. Add the cumin seeds and let them sizzle for 3–4 seconds. Add the dried red chili peppers, curry leaves, garlic, ginger, green chili peppers, tomatoes, and Asian red chili powder or cayenne pepper. Cook, stirring constantly, for 1 minute. Add the cooked lentils and pumpkin to this mixture. Mix well, adding more water as needed. The consistency should be like a soft porridge. Taste for seasoning and add salt if needed.

Stir in the fresh coriander leaves and lime juice. Transfer to a serving bowl, serve hot.

Chapter 5 VEGETABLES AND CHEESE

The trend toward a healthy lifestyle is steering many of us to join the "Vegetarian Revolution." And people interested in low-fat food are looking for great flavor, delectable appearance, and wide variety in the foods that they eat. This is where Indian cuisine really shines! Indian food has unique, interesting, and strong flavors derived from spices, seasonings, and nutritious ingredients such as leafy vegetables, grains, fruits, and legumes. Typically, vegetables are either braised or sautéed, combined with garlic and spices, and served with rice or curries.

For vegetarians and meat eaters alike, vegetable dishes are a key part of every Indian meal. Indians have truly perfected the art of vegetarian cooking. From the simplest of vegetables, they create a mouth-watering variety of food. A fixture in most parts of India, a typical *thali* is a seemingly endless procession of vegetable dish samples—sometimes with unlimited servings. These include vegetables cooked in aromatic spices, a variety of crisp fried snacks, staples like rice and rotis, and an array of delectable confections. You can mix up several simple vegetables mentioned in this chapter in small portions and delight your guests and family with a *thali* dinner on any special occasion!

Paneer is a fresh cheese common in Indian cuisine. In eastern parts of Indian subcontinent, it is generally called *chhena*. It is an unaged, acid-set, non-melting farmer cheese or curd cheese made by curdling heated milk with lemon juice, vinegar, or any other food acid. Dating back to ancient India, paneer remains the most common type of cheese in traditional Indian cuisine. It is also used for making sweets and desserts in some parts of the country. The use of paneer is also common in Nepal, Pakistan, and Bangladesh owing to the prominence of milk in their cuisines.

Pan-Roasted Sweet Potatoes with Coconut
Shakkar Kandi aur Nariyal ki Subzi

I discovered this recipe while I was planning a menu for friends who were visiting me for Thanksgiving. I wanted to make something different with the sweet potatoes and so I dished out this variation, which was very well appreciated by my guests. The spices and the coconut give the mashed sweet potatoes a special Indian twist. Use this during the holidays to fish for compliments. If you are making this for an Indian meal, serve it with dal and *chapati*.

Serves 4
Prep time: **15 minutes**
Cook time: **30 minutes**

2 tablespoons oil
½ teaspoon cumin seeds
1 teaspoon fennel seeds
2 dried red chili peppers, broken in half
6 fresh or dried curry leaves
1 onion (about 5 oz/150 g), chopped
1 lb (500 g) sweet potatoes, cut into 2-in (5-cm) sticks
1 teaspoon ground coriander
1 teaspoon light brown sugar
Salt, to taste
1 cup (100 g) shredded unsweetened coconut (frozen, reconstituted dried, or freshly grated) (see page 14)
¼ cup (65 ml) water
4 tablespoons minced fresh coriander leaves (cilantro), for garnish

Heat the oil in a large, heavy skillet over medium-high heat. Add the cumin, fennel, red chili peppers, and curry leaves and fry briefly until fragrant. Add the onion and cook, stirring frequently, until golden brown, about 5 minutes.

Add the sweet potatoes. Lower the heat to medium and cook, stirring constantly to prevent sticking, for 5 minutes. Add the ground coriander, brown sugar, and salt. Cook until the sweet potato is softened, about 15 minutes.

Add the coconut and stir to break up lumps and blend it into the sweet potato mixture. Add the water, if needed, and cook an additional 2–3 minutes, stirring to prevent sticking. Taste for seasoning and add more salt if necessary. Garnish with the chopped fresh coriander leaves.

Fresh Pineapple Curry
Ananas Huli

This dish is inspired by, and often served at, traditional weddings in southwest India. This sweet curry can be made using pineapples or mangoes to balance all the flavors. It encapsulates the flavors so important to Indians. An everyday menu might be simple, have and just three or four courses, but will range from a bitter dish to a sweeter one. This particular curry is used mostly in the cuisines of Kerala and Mangalore.

Serves 4
Prep time: 15 minutes
Cook time: 20 minutes

1 lb (500 g) fresh pineapple, peeled, cored, and diced 1-in (2.5-cm) pieces
1 teaspoon ground mustard
¼ teaspoon ground turmeric
2–3 teaspoons sugar (depending on the sourness of the pineapple)
1 teaspoon salt
½ cup (50 g) shredded coconut (fresh or frozen)
2 fresh green chili peppers
1 teaspoon tamarind paste
1 cup (250 ml) water
2 tablespoons oil
1 teaspoon mustard seeds

10–12 fresh curry leaves
2 dried red chili peppers, broken into pieces
½ cup (125 ml) coconut milk
2 tablespoons chopped coriander leaves (cilantro)

Put the pineapple pieces, ground mustard, turmeric, sugar, and half the salt in a medium mixing bowl. Mix well. Leave to marinade for about 15–30 minutes.

Put the coconut, green chilies, tamarind paste, remaining salt, and water into a blender and purée until smooth. Set aside.

Heat the oil in a shallow pan over medium heat. When hot, add the mustard seeds and let them splutter. Add the curry leaves and red chili peppers, stirring constantly for about a minute. Add the pineapple.

Stir-fry for about 8–10 minutes.

Add the puréed coconut mixture and the coconut milk and mix well. Taste for seasoning and adjust the salt and sugar if necessary. The dish should have a perfect balance of sweet, sour, salt, and spice. Simmer for about 5 minutes. Garnish with the chopped coriander leaves before serving.

Kerala-Style Mixed Vegetable Curry **Avial**

This is a take on the very popular dish from Kerala called *avial*. You can use any seasonal vegetables for this dish. Some unconventional ingredients that are typically used in this dish are drumstick tree pods, plantains, and sweet potatoes. In India, coconut oil is primarily used in this dish for its unique flavor, but any vegetable oil can be used. Serve with steaming hot rice.

Serves 4
Prep time: **20 minutes**
Cook time: **20 minutes**

1 red onion (about 5 oz/150 g), coarsely chopped
¼ cup (25 g) shredded unsweetened coconut, fresh or frozen
3 tablespoons plus 2 cups (500 ml) water
1 handful fresh coriander (cilantro) leaves and stems (about 3½/100 g) plus 4 tablespoons minced fresh coriander leaves (cilantro)
2 fresh green chili peppers
¼ cup (65 ml) oil
12 shallots (about 3½/100 g total), peeled and cut into wedges
10 fresh or dried curry leaves
1 piece fresh ginger, ½-in (1.25-cm), peeled and chopped

2 or 3 cloves garlic, crushed
2 fresh green chili peppers, slit into half with stems removed
1 teaspoon salt, plus more if needed
½ teaspoon ground turmeric
1 teaspoon ground coriander
1 teaspoon ground cumin
½ cup (60 g) green peas, fresh or frozen
¼ lb (125 g) fresh green beans, trimmed and cut into 1-in (2.5-cm) lengths
1 cup (175 g) broccoli florets or 1 cup (100 g) cauliflower florets
1 carrot, peeled and cut into 1-in (2.5-cm) lengths
1 small potato, peeled and cut into 1-in (2.5-cm) lengths (about ¾ cup/130 g)
2 cups (500 ml) coconut milk

Place the red onion, coconut, 3 tablespoons of water, handful of fresh coriander leaves with stems, and green chili peppers in a blender or food processor and process to a smooth paste. Set aside.

Heat the oil in a large saucepan over medium heat. Add the shallots, curry leaves, ginger, garlic, and green chili peppers and fry for 2–3 minutes, stirring constantly, until soft. Add the coconut paste and salt and cook, uncovered, stirring frequently, for about 5 minutes.

Add the turmeric, coriander, cumin, and all the vegetables and fry for another minute. Add the 2 cups (500 ml) of water and cover. Cook, stirring occasionally, for 15–20 minutes or until the vegetables are tender.

Add the coconut milk and minced fresh coriander leaves. Mix well and taste for seasoning, adding more salt if needed. Serve hot.

Spicy Long Beans and Potato Stir-Fry Alsande Batate Poriyal

Long beans are not readily available in American grocery stores, but they can be found in Chinese or Asian markets. You can use regular French beans as well. I love the combination of mustard seeds, shredded coconut, and vegetables in this dish. *Poriyals* are a type of lightly seasoned sautéed, or "dry," vegetable dishes from southern India. They emphasize the flavor of fresh vegetables cooked in their own juices and moisture. Serve this dish alongside the Whole Wheat Griddle Bread (page 122) or the Brown Basmati Rice (page 119) for a simple weekday meal.

Serves 6
Prep time: **10 minutes**
Cook time: **15 minutes**

4 tablespoons oil
3 teaspoons black mustard seeds
1 piece fresh ginger, 1-in (2.5-cm), peeled and chopped
1 tablespoon minced garlic
2 teaspoons cumin seeds
4 dried red chili peppers
10 fresh curry leaves
1 lb (500 g) Chinese long beans, trimmed and cut into 2-in (5-cm) lengths
1 large potato, peeled and cut into 2-in (5-cm) lengths
1 teaspoon ground coriander
¼ teaspoon ground turmeric
1¼ teaspoons salt
1 cup (100 g) shredded unsweetened coconut (frozen, reconstituted dried, or freshly grated) (see page 14)
1 cup (250 ml) water
Juice of ½ lemon

Heat the oil in a wide, heavy pot over medium heat. When hot, add the mustard seeds and cook, stirring constantly, until they splutter and pop, about 30 seconds. Immediately add the ginger, garlic, cumin seeds, red chili peppers, and curry leaves and cook, stirring constantly, for about 1 minute. Add the beans, potato, coriander, turmeric, salt, and coconut and cook, stirring frequently, for 3–4 minutes, until fragrant.

Add the water and bring to a simmer. Cover and cook until the beans are tender, about 7–10 minutes. Remove the cover, add the lemon juice and cook, stirring often, until all of the water is evaporated. Taste for seasoning and add more salt if necessary. Serve hot.

Scrambled Paneer with Chilies Paneer Bhurji

This is an all-time Café Spice office favorite! Sameer often brings in this quick-tossed homemade *paneer bhurji* and eats it during a working lunch on a busy day at the office. When he brings some that combines egg and paneer, I never miss an opportunity to share it with him!

Serves 4
Prep time: 20 minutes
Cook time: 15 minutes

3 tablespoons oil
1 tablespoon minced garlic
2 fresh green chili peppers, slit open lengthwise
1 tablespoon plus 1 teaspoon peeled and minced fresh ginger
1 red onion (about 4 oz/125 g), thinly sliced
¼ teaspoon ground turmeric
1 teaspoon Café Spice Garam Masala (page 22)
1 green bell pepper, thinly sliced
1 lb (500 g) Paneer Cheese (page 76), grated
Salt, to taste
4 tablespoons minced fresh coriander leaves (cilantro)
Juice of ½ lime

SPICE BLEND
6 dried red chili peppers
1 tablespoon plus 1 teaspoon coriander seeds
1 tablespoon plus 1 teaspoon cumin seeds

To make the Spice Blend: Grind the red chili peppers, coriander, and cumin seeds in a spice grinder to make a coarse powder. Set aside.

Heat the oil in a wok or a saucepan over medium heat. Add the minced garlic and fry until light brown, about a minute. Add the green chili peppers, ginger, and onion and sauté for 30 seconds. Then add the Spice Blend and cook for 30 seconds, stirring constantly.

Add the green pepper and cook over medium heat for 30 seconds. Add the grated paneer, stirring gently for 2–3 minutes. Sprinkle with the salt, fresh coriander leaves, and lime juice. Stir and serve hot.

VARIATION: ANDA PANEER BHURGI—Eggs, or *anda* in Hindi, are a commonly used ingredient in Indian cooking. To make this dish simply add 3 hard-boiled eggs, grated or chopped, to the above recipe. This is a delicious variation that goes well with Whole Wheat Griddle Bread (page 122).

Baby Corn and Green Beans Beans Corn Thoran

This dish is inspired by the popularity of using baby corn as an ingredient in Asian cuisine. Green beans are a popular and quick choice for a vegetable dish in many kitchens in India. This is my version, where I have added baby corns. Fresh baby corn work best for this recipe, but canned baby corn works nearly as well.

Serves 6
Prep time: **10 minutes**
Cook time: **15 minutes**

4 tablespoons oil
3 teaspoons black mustard seeds
1 tablespoon Ginger Garlic Paste (page 22)
2 teaspoons cumin seeds
4 dried red chili peppers
10 fresh or dried curry leaves
8 oz (250 g) green beans, preferably thin French beans, trimmed and cut on the diagonal into 1-in (2.5-cm) lengths
8 oz (250 g) baby corn, fresh or canned, trimmed and cut on the diagonal into 1-in (2.5-cm) lengths
1 teaspoon Café Spice Garam Masala (page 22)
¼ teaspoon ground turmeric
1¼ teaspoons salt
2 tablespoons chopped coriander leaves (cilantro)
Juice of ½ lemon

Heat the oil in a wide, heavy pot over medium heat. When hot, add the mustard seeds and cook, stirring constantly, until they splutter and pop, about 30 seconds. Immediately add the Ginger-Garlic Paste, cumin seeds, red chili peppers, and curry leaves and cook, stirring constantly, for about 1 minute. Add the beans, baby corn, Garam Masala, turmeric, salt, and cook, stirring frequently for 3–4 minutes, until fragrant.

Add a little water if needed to ensure faster cooking (optional). Cover and cook until the beans are tender, about 7–10 minutes. Remove the cover; add the coriander leaves, and lemon juice and cook, stirring often, until all of the water is evaporated. Taste for seasoning and add more salt if necessary. Serve hot.

Smoky Fire-Roasted Eggplant Baingan Bharta

I love the smoky aroma and taste of this eggplant delicacy, which is cooked with onions, tomatoes, and spices, and served over Whole Wheat Griddle Bread (page 122). Though the eggplant is traditionally charcoal-smoked, the smoking can also be done over a gas burner on a stove top or under the broiler. The eggplants used in this recipe are not the usual ones found in the regular grocery. These long, slim, perfectly purple eggplants are usually found in an Asian or an Indian grocery store and deliver a slightly different flavor from the usual ones, when cooked. This preparation is rather simple and healthy, yet the use of cumin and green chilies makes it really tasty. This dish can easily be rolled up in Indian flatbreads, or a store-bought wrap for a perfect meal-on-the-go.

Serves 4
Prep time: 10 minutes
Cook time: 30 minutes

4 baby eggplants (Asian or Italian) or 2 large eggplants (globe variety), about 2½ lbs (1 kg) total
¾ cup (185 ml) ghee (clarified butter) or oil
1 teaspoon cumin seeds
1 red onion (about 5 oz/150 g), finely chopped
1 piece fresh ginger, 1-in (2.5-cm), peeled and chopped
1 teaspoon paprika
Salt, to taste
2 tomatoes (about ¾ lb/350 g), chopped
3 fresh green chili peppers, minced
4 tablespoons chopped fresh coriander leaves (cilantro)

Preheat a grill to medium heat or a broiler to 325°F (160°C) and set the oven rack 5 inches (12.5 cm) below the heat source.

Flame-char the whole eggplants on the gas grill, turning constantly, until blackened and soft, about 15 minutes. Alternatively, you may roast the eggplants under the preheated broiler on a sheet pan until completely soft and lightly burnt and the skin starts peeling off, about 15–20 minutes.

Immerse the grilled or roasted eggplants in cold water to cool. Remove the skin and stem and coarsely chop the flesh. (You should have nearly 2 cups/500 g chopped eggplant.) Set aside.

Heat the ghee or oil in a saucepan over medium heat. Add the cumin and sauté until it begins to crackle, about 30 seconds. Add the onion and cook until transparent, about 2 minutes. Add the ginger and cook, stirring constantly, for 30 seconds.

Reduce the heat to medium-low. Add the paprika, salt, and tomatoes and cook until the fat starts to leave the sides, about 2 minutes. Add the chopped eggplant and green chili peppers and cook, stirring constantly, until soft and mushy, about 4–5 minutes. Stir in the chopped coriander leaves and serve hot.

TIP: When selecting eggplants, choose ones that are shiny and seem light for their size. They will have fewer seeds.

Okra Masala Bhindi Subzi

Okra is simply divine with any Indian meal. If you have previously cooked okra and ended up with slimy results, you may be discouraged from making it at home. But don't be! You need only follow my aunt's three cardinal rules: Always wipe okra dry before cutting it, always cook it without a lid, and do not stir it too much while cooking. Following her tips will ensure that the okra does not have a slimy texture. If you prefer okra crispy, deep-frying is a good option. Always pick out the smallest okra as they will be the most tender. Frozen, cut okra may be used when fresh is out of season. Serve this as a side dish with a saucy curry or a dal and some *chapati* (page 122) or rice of your choice.

Serves 4
Prep time: **15 minutes**
Cook time: **15 minutes**

1 lb (500 g) fresh tender okra,
   rinsed and patted dry or
   1 lb (500 g) cut, frozen okra
½ cup (125 ml) oil
2 teaspoons cumin seeds
1 large onion (about 8 oz/
   250 g), sliced
½ teaspoon ground coriander
½ teaspoon ground cumin
½ teaspoon Asian red chili
   powder or cayenne pepper
¼ teaspoon ground turmeric
½ teaspoon salt
1 small tomato (about 3 oz/
   85 g), chopped
Juice of ½ lemon

Trim the ends off each okra and cut the pod into small segments, approximately ½-in (1.25-cm) in length.

Heat the oil in a nonstick skillet over medium-high heat. Add the cumin seeds—they should sizzle on contact with the hot oil. Quickly add the onion and cook, stirring frequently, until golden, about 3–4 minutes. Add the okra and fry, stirring every now and then, for 10 minutes.

The onion will be dark brown by this time. Add the ground spices, salt, and tomato and sauté for another 5 minutes. Add the lemon juice and cook, stirring gently, for another minute. Serve hot.

Stir-Fried Spinach and Red Chard Palak Subzi

I never liked Swiss chard until a few years ago when I had some that had been freshly picked from a garden. It was so sweet and buttery I couldn't believe it was actually the same vegetable. It was then that I learned that freshness is the key factor that determines whether chard is delectable or detestable. Store-bought chard can be quite good, but not nearly as fantastic as the chard bought at the farmer's market. So here's a hint. If the thought of Swiss chard leaves you uninspired, get some that has been freshly picked. It is sort of like the difference between sweeet corn picked that day, and the same corn two days later. The flavors cannot be compared.

Serves 4
Prep time: **15 minutes**
Cook time: **30 minutes**

2 tablespoons vegetable oil
1¼ teaspoons cumin seeds
½ teaspoon fennel seeds
1 teaspoon peeled minced ginger
1 tablespoon peeled minced garlic
1 fresh green chili pepper, minced
1 teaspoon ground turmeric
½ lb (250 g) spinach leaves,
    washed and tough stalks
    stems and chopped
8 oz (250 g) red Swiss chard,
    washed and chopped, tough
    stalks removed
Salt, to taste
½ teaspoon sugar
½ cup (10 g) fresh coriander
    leaves (cilantro), including
    soft stems, chopped
¼ teaspoon Café Spice Garam
    Masala (page 22)

Heat the oil in a large saucepan over medium-high heat and add the cumin and fennel seeds; they should sizzle on contact with the hot oil. Quickly add the ginger, garlic, green chili peppers, and ground turmeric and cook, stirring, about 2 minutes.

Add the spinach and swiss chard leaves and salt, cover the pan, and cook, stirring as needed, over medium-high heat for 2–3 minutes, then reduce the heat to medium-low and cook until the chard is tender, about 5 minutes.

Mix in the fresh coriander leaves. Transfer to a serving bowl, sprinkle the Garam Masala on top, and serve.

Paneer Cheese

Paneer, which is also known as Indian cottage cheese, is made by curdling milk with something acid, lemon juice or vinegar, and then separating the curds from the whey. This soft, spongy cheese, with its sweet and milky aroma is preservative-free, has no artificial additives, and can be made with low-fat or whole milk. Paneer does not need to be used only in Indian dishes. *Note*: The paneer recipes in this chapter require twice the amount of paneer that this recipe makes. If you have a pot large enough to hold two gallons of milk, with sufficient headroom, I recommend that you make a double batch. Otherwise, simply make the recipe twice.

Prep time: **10 minutes**
Cook time: **30 minutes**
Makes ½ lb (250 g)

1 gallon (3.75 liters) low-fat or whole milk
1 cup (250 ml) freshly squeezed lemon juice
    (4–6 lemons) or white vinegar
1 square piece of fine muslin, 3-foot
    (1-meter) or 4 layers of cheesecloth

VARIATION: FLAVORED PANEER CHEESE—
Paneer cheese can also be made with about 1 cup (200 g) chopped, fresh herbs like basil, tarragon, or mint. Or, you may add about 2 tablespoons of toasted cumin seeds or toasted fennel seeds to the above recipe to give it a different texture and flavor. Store in an airtight container in the refrigerator 4–5 days or freeze up to 4 months.

Place the milk in a large, heavy saucepan and bring to a boil, stirring constantly, over medium-high heat. As soon as the milk comes to a boil, add the lemon juice and lower the heat to medium. Continue to stir until the milk curdles and separates into curds, which resemble cottage cheese, and whey, 1–2 minutes. Remove from the heat. Let it sit for 5 minutes.

Drape the muslin or cheesecloth over a large pan and pour the curdled milk over it. As you do this, the whey drains through the cloth into the pan, and curdled paneer cheese remains in the cloth. Tie the ends of the cloth together and hang over a sink to drain. Allow to drain 3–5 minutes.

Twist the cloth around the cheese, and then place the cheese between two plates. Place a large pan of water or a heavy saucepan on the top plate and let the cheese drain further, 10–20 minutes.

Remove the weight off the cheese (which, by now, should have compressed into a chunk), cut into desired shapes and sizes, and use as needed. Store in an airtight container in the refrigerator 4–5 days or freeze up to 4 months.

Paneer with Creamed Spinach Palak Paneer

Anyone who has been to an Indian restaurant has probably tasted *palak* or *saag paneer*. The two words describe a popular combination of spinach, cubed fresh cheese, and curry spices that is commonly eaten with flat bread or rice. With the addition of cream or milk to temper spicy seasonings, saag paneer makes for a well-balanced contrast of textures and flavors that magically masks the individual spices contained in this curry. (You may not able to identify each flavor, but your taste buds will love how they combine.) Paneer is easily and affordably made at home in reasonable time (Paneer Cheese, page 76). Started in the morning, your non-melting fresh cheese becomes a softer, blander counterpoint to the heat of the curry blend. For a homestyle effect, use the spinach chopped, instead of puréeing it. This recipe calls for puréed spinach to duplicate the presentation of your favorite restaurant-style saag paneer.

Serves 4
Prep time: 40 minutes
Cook time: 40 minutes

2½ lbs (1 kg) spinach, washed and tough stems removed
½ cup (50 g) dried fenugreek leaves, chopped (optional)
3½ tablespoons oil
1 teaspoon minced garlic
½ cup (125 ml) tomato purée
½ teaspoon Asian red chili powder or cayenne pepper
¼ teaspoon ground turmeric
½ teaspoon ground coriander
1 teaspoon salt, or to taste
1 cup (250 ml) water
1 cup (250 ml) cream
½ teaspoon Café Spice Garam Masala (page 22)
2 teaspoons dried fenugreek leaves (*kasoori methi*), crushed (optional)
1 lb (500 g) Paneer Cheese (page 76) diced

Bring a large saucepan of water to a boil. Place the spinach and fenugreek leaves in the boiling water and cook until just done, about 3 minutes. Drain in a colander and rinse under cold water. Purée the spinach and fenugreek in a blender or a food processor until smooth, adding a little water if necessary. Set aside.

Heat the oil in a skillet over medium heat. Add the garlic and sauté for 30 seconds, until slightly brown. Add the spinach purée and cook, while stirring, for about 2 minutes. Add the tomato purée, Asian red chili powder or cayenne pepper, turmeric, coriander, salt, and water. Cook for about 5 minutes. Stir in the cream, Garam Masala, and dried fenugreek leaves. And the diced Paneer Cheese and let simmer for about 3–5 minutes, gently stirring from time to time. Remove from the heat. Serve hot.

Chapter 6 FISH AND SEAFOOD

Seafood is very popular in India and a staple of coastal India. It is often eaten by some communities in which people call themselves "vegetarian!" Like any other ingredient, fish is cooked in thousands of different ways.

In the north, it is dipped in batters and fried or cooked in a tandoor oven. In the south it is prepared with tamarind, curry leaves, and fenugreek. From the east there's *doi maach* (Bengali Fish Curry, page 88) or fish cooked with yogurt. From the west there are delicious coconut-based curries (Goan-Style Mackerel, page 89). For a country with a vast coastline, fish and seafood are a rather natural choice for inhabitants along the coast. In fact, fishing is quite an important occupation among the rural settlers along Indian coastlines. India is also spotted with several fresh-water lakes, ponds, and rivers, which yield sweeter fish because of the naturally lower saline content in the water.

Fish is truly good for you; low in calories and high in protein. Easy to digest and naturally tender, fish cooks quickly no matter which method you use. The most common method of cooking and serving fish and seafood in Indian homes is as a curry—usually accompanied by rice. Other popular techniques are pan-frying and deep-frying. When fish or seafood is pan-fried, it is coated with spices (Pan-Fried Crispy Fish, page 90). When deep-fried, it is coated with a batter or a crust. Baking and grilling is not done very often in homes in India. In restaurants, in addition to the traditional homestyle cooking methods, fish may be baked in a tandoor oven to create tandoori-style fish dishes, or grilled (Grilled Tandoori Fish, page 85).

The majority of the seafood that is available in your local grocery will take well to Indian flavors. Most Indian recipes can be made with varieties of fish that are easy to find in the West, such as sea bass, halibut, salmon, snapper, halibut, haddock, cod, or even swordfish.

Bombay Green Fish Parsi Machhi

This recipe is inspired by Latha's cooking. From the first time that I shared this dish with the family, in the Malhotra residence, I have wanted to recreate it. This version is as close as I can get to the recipe. You can substitute cream of coconut or coconut milk for the grated coconut. A couple helpful tips: Grind the spices and cashew nuts together and add ¾ cup (185 ml) of coconut cream or milk with ¾ cup (185 ml) of water after adding the fresh cilantro leaf mixture. You can use this recipe to make a vegetarian version using 1 lb (500 g) diced mixed vegetables, in which case add 2 cups (500 ml) of water at the end and cook the vegetables until done.

Serves 4
Prep time: **15 minutes**
Cook time: **15 minutes**

Juice of 1 lime
¼ teaspoon ground turmeric
2 teaspoons salt
1½ lbs (750 g) fish fillets or steaks (pomfret, cod, kingfish, mackerel, or snapper) 4 cod
1 tablespoon poppy seeds
1 cup (100 g) shredded unsweetened coconut, fresh or frozen
5 fresh green chili peppers 1 can   ~½ c dry
1 onion (about 4 oz/125 g) chopped
3 cloves garlic
2 tablespoons chopped cashew nuts
1 green cardamom pod
¼ teaspoon ground mace
¼ teaspoon fennel seeds
1 teaspoon coriander seeds ¼ t
1½ cups (60 g) packed fresh coriander (cilantro) leaves and stalks
½ cup (20 g) packed fresh mint leaves
⅓ cup (80 ml) oil
1 teaspoon cumin seeds
1 teaspoon sugar
1¾ cups (425 ml) water

Mix half the lime juice with the turmeric, 1 teaspoon of salt, and a few drops of water in a small bowl and spread evenly over the pieces of fish. Let them sit and marinate for 20 minutes while you prepare the other ingredients.

In a blender, grind together the poppy seeds, coconut, chili peppers, onion, garlic, cashew nuts, cardamom, mace, fennel, coriander seeds, coriander, and mint leaves with ¼ cup (65 ml) of water to make a smooth paste.

Add the oil and cumin seeds in a nonstick saucepan over medium heat. When the cumin seeds begin to splutter, add the coconut and spice paste and sauté for 5–7 minutes, stirring continuously, making sure the mixture does not stick to the pan.

Add the sugar and remaining lime juice. Pour in the remaining water and bring to a boil. Add the fish pieces and cook until done, about 7–10 minutes over low to medium heat depending on the cut and size of the fish. Serve hot.

Spiced Crab Cakes Kekda Tikki

Fresh crab or canned lump crabmeat works well for this recipe. Like Goan Fish Cakes (page 38), this dish can be made in advance, kept frozen, and fried as needed. It is nothing like a common restaurant crab cake. In fact, it is a Western crab cake with an Indian heart! Serve it with an Indianized aioli by mixing chutneys—tamarind or mint—with mayonnaise. I also like to serve it with Spiced Pear Chutney (page 26). If you are willing to go the extra mile, this recipe works best with fresh crabmeat. Make it a part of a special party meal.

Serves 4
Prep time: **15 minutes**
Cook time: **15 minutes**

4 tablespoons oil
1 small red onion (about 4 oz/125 g), minced
1 piece of fresh ginger, 1-in (2.5-cm), peeled minced
1 teaspoon minced garlic
2 teaspoons ground coriander
1 teaspoon Asian red chili powder or cayenne pepper
Salt, to taste
1 teaspoon Café Spice Garam Masala (page 22)
Juice of 1 lime
2 small handfuls fresh coriander (cilantro) leaves and stalks, chopped
3 cups (300 g) crabmeat, freshly prepared or canned
1 egg, whisked
2½ tablespoons mayonnaise
10 slices of thick bread, edges removed and crumbled

Heat 1½ tablespoons of the oil in a medium-size skillet over medium heat and fry the onions for about 4 minutes, until soft. Add the ginger and garlic and cook for another 40 seconds. Stir in the ground coriander, red chili powder, salt, and Garam Masala. Cook for another 20 seconds and then remove from the heat. Add the lime juice, coriander, crabmeat, egg, and mayonnaise. Stir well and add the breadcrumbs. Divide into eight portions and form into patties.

Add 1 tablespoon of oil in a large, wide, nonstick skillet over medium heat, and cook the crab cakes in batches for about 2–3 minutes on each side, until golden. Add the remaining oil when cooking the second batch of cakes. Serve the crab cakes with greens of your choice on the side.

Shrimp and Mango Curry
Kerala Jhinga

This is a wonderful seafood stew with coconut to which I sometimes add firm white fish, mussels, or clams. Serve over rice with a green salad.

Serves 4
Prep time: **15 minutes**
Cook time: **15 minutes**

1 lb (500 g) medium-size shrimp, peeled, deveined
Juice of ½ lime
¾ teaspoon ground turmeric
Salt, to taste
¼ cup (25 g) shredded coconut, fresh or frozen
3 teaspoons coriander seeds
1 onion (about 5 oz/150 g), sliced
1 teaspoon cumin seeds
1½ teaspoons minced garlic
1½ teaspoons tamarind paste
2 tablespoons oil
3 fresh green chili peppers, slit lengthwise
1 mango, not fully ripe (about ½ lb/250 g), peeled, cored and cut into small dice
4 cups (1 liter) water
4 tablespoons chopped fresh coriander leaves (cilantro)

Marinate the shrimp in a mixture of the lime juice, a pinch of the turmeric powder, and salt. Let it sit for about 30 minutes.

In a blender or food processor grind the coconut, coriander seeds, half the sliced onions, cumin seeds, the remaining ground turmeric, garlic, and tamarind paste to make a really fine and smooth paste. Add a little water to facilitate grinding, which will take 7–10 minutes for a really smooth paste.

Heat the oil in a wide large skillet or wok over medium heat. Add the remaining sliced onion and green chili peppers until lightly colored, about 5–7 minutes.

Add the mangoes and spice paste and sauté over moderate heat for 6–7 minutes, adding a little water if necessary to prevent sticking. When the oil begins to separate from the spices in the form of little globules on the surface of the paste, add the water. Add the shrimp and cook until done, about 5 minutes. Sprinkle with the chopped coriander leaves when serving.

Grilled Tandoori Fish Tandoori Macchi

I have noticed several brands that have started producing tandoori masalas and selling them through retail outlets in the USA. If you are in a hurry, you can use one of these preparations rather than making it from scratch. These skewered morsels make for a great party snack because of the pretty presentation they make. Place them over a salad, if serving them like an appetizer, or pair with Brown Basmati Rice (page 119) and make them a meal.

Serves 4
Prep time: **15 minutes**
Cook time: **15 minutes**

2 tablespoons chickpea (besan) or rice flour
4 tablespoons plain yogurt, whisked
Juice of ½ lime
1 teaspoon ground turmeric,
1 teaspoon Asian red chili powder or cayenne pepper
1 teaspoon paprika
1 teaspoon Café Spice Garam Masala (page 22)
3 tablespoons Ginger-Garlic Paste (page 22)
1 tablespoon oil
Salt, to taste
1½ lbs (750 g) firm fish fillet (monk fish, mahi-mahi, or
    swordfish), cut into large cubes
4 bamboo skewers, 12-in (30-cm), soaked in water for 1 hour
2 tablespoons melted butter, to baste
Lemon wedges, to serve

Mix together all the ingredients for the marinade: chickpea flour, yogurt, lime juice, spices, Ginger-Garlic Paste, oil, and salt in a small bowl. Rub well into the fish and leave to marinate in a covered bowl in the refrigerator for 1–2 hours. Bring back to room temperature before cooking.

Preheat the grill to high heat. If broiling the fish, preheat the broiler to high heat and set the oven rack 4 inches (10 cm) below the heat source. Thread the fish onto the skewers, place on a buttered baking sheet and bake for 10 minutes in the middle of the oven. Baste the fish with the melted butter and cook for another 3–4 minutes. Serve with lemon wedges and green salad of your choice.

Scallops with Coconut and Ginger Curry

This dish is best with steamed rice on the side. It is a take on a very popular Kerala dish called "fish *moilee*." Make it to impress someone special as it really is a beautiful dish. If you are lucky enough to find fresh scallops with the roe intact, don't take them off before cooking. Leave them on like I do; they taste very good with the sauce.

Serves 4
Prep time: **15 minutes**
Cook time: **15–20 minutes**

3 tablespoons oil
10 fresh curry leaves
1 onion (about 5 oz/150 g), sliced
1 piece fresh ginger,1-in (2.5-cm), peeled and cut into thin strips
4 fresh green chili peppers, slit open lengthwise
½ teaspoon ground turmeric
2 cups (500 ml) coconut milk
2 teaspoons salt
16 large sea scallops (about 1¼ lbs/ 600 g), gently rinsed and blotted dry with paper towels
1 teaspoon toasted and coarsely ground coriander seeds
1 teaspoon toasted and coarsely ground cumin seeds
½ teaspoon crushed red pepper

For the sauce:
First make the sauce. Heat 1 tablespoon of the oil in a large skillet over medium heat. Add the curry leaves, onion, ginger, and green chili peppers and cook, stirring until the onion is soft, about 5 minutes.

Add the turmeric, followed by the coconut milk and 1 teaspoon of salt and bring to a simmer. Cook for 3–5 minutes until the sauce begins to turn glossy and thickens enough to coat the back of a spoon lightly. Set aside.

Heat the remaining oil in a large, heavy-bottomed skillet over high heat, add the scallops and sear for about 1 minute per side, until golden brown. Move the pan off the heat. Sprinkle the remaining salt on both sides of the scallops.

Mix together the coriander seeds, cumin seeds, and the crushed red pepper and spread on the scallops to give an even crust. Place the pan back on heat and cook for another 30 seconds on each side. Serve with the coconut sauce.

Lobster Kadhai

A fantastic way to present this dish for a special occasion is to serve it right in the lobster shells. This dish is a showstopper! Although it requires patience to process the whole lobster, it is worth all the effort if your aim is to impress someone! To serve it in the beautiful red shell, simply dry the shells out first by putting them in a warm oven for 5–6 minutes until bright red. Serve the cooked lobster meat by spooning it into the shells. Alternatively, if you do not want to deal with the whole live lobsters, you can replace two whole lobsters with four tails, about 8 oz (225 g) each, which are easily available fresh or frozen in the supermarket.

Serves 4
Prep time: 30 minutes
Cook time: 20 minutes

2 live medium size lobsters, about 1½ lbs (750 g)
4 tablespoons vegetable oil
2 green cardamom pods
1 cinnamon stick, 1-in (2.5-cm)
1 teaspoon cumin seeds, coarsely crushed
1 teaspoon coriander seeds, coarsely crushed
1 teaspoon fennel seeds, coarsely crushed
1 large white onion (about 8 oz/250 g), chopped
1 tablespoon minced garlic
1 piece fresh ginger, 1-in (2.5-cm), peeled and minced
2 teaspoons Asian red chili powder or cayenne pepper
4 tomatoes (about 1 lb/500 g), finely chopped
1½ teaspoons salt
½ teaspoon Café Spice Garam Masala (page 22)
1 tablespoon butter
1 small red onion (about 4 oz/125 g), diced
½ red pepper (about 4 oz/125 g), seeded and diced
½ fresh yellow bell pepper (about 4 oz/125 g), seeded and diced
4 fresh green chili peppers, slit open
1 teaspoon crushed red pepper
½ teaspoon freshly cracked black peppercorns
1 tablespoon heavy cream
1 teaspoon dried fenugreek leaves, crushed with your fingertips
Juice of ½ lemon
4 tablespoons chopped fresh coriander leaves (cilantro)

Place the lobsters in the freezer for about 2 hours, this will ensure that they are not moving. Then plunge them into a large pan of boiling water and simmer for 2–3 minutes. Remove from the pan and place them in a large bowl of ice for about 10–15 minutes, until chilled.

Hold the lobster in one hand and using a strong heavy knife, cut each lobster lengthwise in half. Remove the flesh from the shell. Twist the claws off the body and crack them using the heel of the knife. Remove the claw meat from the shells and set aside. Cut the body meat into a ½-in (1.25-cm) dice and set aside.

Heat the oil in a heavy-bottomed skillet, add the cardamom, cinnamon, cumin, coriander, and fennel seeds and let them crackle. Add the chopped onions and sauté until golden brown and then add the garlic, ginger, and red chili powder and sauté for 1–2 minutes. Now add the chopped tomatoes and cook for 4–6 minutes until the tomatoes are soft and a smooth sauce is formed. Stir in the salt and Garam Masala, remove from the heat and set aside. Purée this mixture with a hand-held blender for a smoother sauce (optional).

In a separate heavy-duty nonstick pan, over medium heat, add the butter and sear the lobster claw meat until lightly colored all over. Add the diced red onions, peppers, and green chilies and sauté for about 2–3 minutes, until softened. Add the diced lobster meat and sauté over a high heat for another minute. Add the crushed red pepper and cracked pepper and then pour in the cooked masala, simmer for 2–3 minutes. Check the seasoning and add more salt if needed. Stir in the cream, fenugreek, lemon juice, and chopped coriander. Serve hot.

Bengali Fish Curry **Doi Maach**

During my travels and research for an upcoming book on India, I was fortunate to have been able to stay with a friend who hails from Kolkata. Her mother taught me how to make this dish the traditional way, in her kitchen. *Doi maach* literally means yogurt fish; this is a take on the classic. It is quite easy to prepare and goes well with rice. Keep in mind that firm fish needs to be used for this preparation. Use halibut, monkfish, cod, or swordfish. Mustard oil is the traditional medium, and the best way to cook any Bengali food. Regular oil can be used as well, and you can follow a trick I use to approximate the flavor of mustard oil: Squeeze a teaspoon of French mustard into the yogurt mixture!

Serves 4
Prep time: **15 minutes**
Cook time: **15 minutes**

2 cups (500 g) plain yogurt, whisked
1 teaspoon Asian red chili powder or cayenne pepper
1 teaspoon ground turmeric
2 tablespoons Ginger-Garlic Paste (page 22)
2½ lbs (1 kg) firm white fish, skinned and cut into 2-in (5-cm) pieces
4 tablespoons mustard oil
1 teaspoon mustard seeds
3 cloves
2 green cardamom pods
1 teaspoon black peppercorns
1 bay leaf
1 large onion (about 8 oz/250 g), chopped
1 teaspoon salt
4 fresh green chili peppers, slit open lengthwise
2 tablespoons chopped fresh coriander leaves (cilantro)

Combine 1 cup of the yogurt, chili powder, turmeric, and Ginger-Garlic Paste in a medium bowl. Add the fish and mix gently until they are well coated. Set aside to marinate for at least 30 minutes.

Heat 3 tablespoons of mustard oil in a large, heavy-bottomed saucepan over medium heat. Add the mustard seeds, cloves, cardamom, peppercorns, and bay leaf and stir-fry for about 30 seconds until the mustard seeds start to splutter.

Add the onion and fry for another 3–4 minutes, until translucent. Add the fish along with the marinade and mix gently to incorporate. Cook for 3–4 minutes. Add the salt, green chilies, and remaining yogurt and cook over medium heat for 8–10 minutes until the fish is cooked.

Garnish with fresh coriander leaves and drizzle the remaining mustard oil on top. Serve hot.

Goan-Style Mackerel Bangda Curry

This is a traditional recipe usually made with mackerel. It is not very complicated to make, and more importantly, it tastes best when consumed the next day. If you can get a traditional clay-pot to cook this dish, the taste is earthy and even more delicious. Goa is the land of beaches and seafood. In India, I have tasted many types of fish curry. While all of them are served with plain white rice, the flavors varied slightly or sometimes distinctly from one another. Here, I have tried to recreate my favorite flavors. It is served best with basmati rice, but a crusty baguette does well for dipping into its smooth velvety sauce.

Serves 4
Prep time: **15 minutes**
Cook time: **15 minutes**

1 lb (500 g) fish steaks
Juice of ½ lime
¾ teaspoon ground turmeric
Salt, to taste
8 red chili peppers
5 cups (1.2 liters) water
1½ teaspoons paprika
¼ cup (25 g) shredded coconut, fresh or frozen
3 teaspoons coriander seeds
1 onion (about 5 oz/150 g), sliced
1 teaspoon cumin seeds
1½ teaspoons minced garlic
1½ teaspoons tamarind paste
2 tablespoons oil
1 large tomato (about 8 oz/250 g), minced
3 fresh green chili peppers, slit lengthwise
4 tablespoons chopped fresh coriander leaves (cilantro)

Marinate the fish in a mixture of the lime juice, a pinch of the turmeric powder, and salt. Let it sit for about 30 minutes.

Soak the red chilies in 1 cup (250 ml) of water for 15 minutes. Strain and reserve the soaking water. In a blender or food processor, grind the soaked chilies, paprika, coconut, coriander seeds, half the sliced onions, cumin seeds, the remaining ground turmeric, garlic, and tamarind pulp to make a really fine and smooth paste. Add a little of the chili soaking water to facilitate grinding, which will take 7–10 minutes for a really smooth paste.

Heat the oil in a wide, large skillet or wok over medium heat. Add the remaining sliced onion until it is lightly colored, about 5–7 minutes.

Add the spice paste and sauté over moderate heat for 6–7 minutes, adding a little water if necessary to prevent sticking. When the oil begins to separate from the spices in the form of little globules on the surface of the paste, add 4 cups (1 liter) of water. Add the tomato, green chilies, and salt to taste and cook for 5 minutes. Add the fish and cook until it is done, about 5–8 minutes. Sprinkle with cilantro leaves when serving.

Pan-Fried Crispy Fish Rawa Meen

Semolina crusted fish is a delicacy belonging mostly to the western coast of India. Beach shacks or small, family-run restaurants serve this with a special homemade red masala. This is my take on the classic dish. The semolina provides a unique texture to the outer coat, balancing the fiery spices that we use to coat the fish. instead of the semolina, you can use dried coconut or Japanese bread crumbs (panko) as a more readily available option to crust it. Serve this along with a glass of chilled beer for a perfect drink pairing.

Serves 4
Prep time: 15 minutes
Cook time: 10 minutes

2 dried red chili peppers, broken
1 piece fresh ginger, ½-in (1.25-cm), peeled and chopped
4 large cloves garlic, peeled and roughly chopped
1 tablespoon white wine vinegar
3 teaspoons ground coriander
6 fenugreek seeds
Salt, to taste
1 teaspoon freshly ground black pepper
¼ cup (65 ml) oil
Four halibut steaks or fillets (about 6 oz/175 g each) or other firm white fish like cod or bass, skin removed
½ cup (75 g) semolina
¼ cup (30 g) rice flour
3 tablespoons oil
Lemon wedges, to serve

In a blender or using a mortar and pestle grind together the red chili, ginger, garlic, vinegar, coriander, fenugreek, salt, pepper, and 1 tablespoon of oil to make a fine purée. Place the fish in this marinade, cover, and leave for at least 30 minutes.

Mix together semolina and the flour on a large plate. Remove the fish from the marinade and place it on the mixture of flour. Press on all sides and coat, creating a generous coating of the dry mixture all over the fish.

Heat the remaining oil in a large nonstick saucepan over medium heat. When hot, add the fish. Cook on low heat without moving the fish for four minutes, then turn over and cook on the other side for another 3–4 minutes or until done. Serve hot with lemon wedges and mixed greens.

Pan-Fried Snapper

This makes an exquisite presentation and can be served as a plated, individual course. As fillet of snapper cooks very quickly, it's best to make this dish at the last minute. You can make the sauce ahead of time and refrigerate it before you serve this dish.

Serves 4
Prep time: 15 minutes
Cook time: 15–20 minutes

3 tablespoons oil
10 fresh curry leaves
1 red onion (about 5 oz/150 g), sliced
1 piece fresh ginger, 1-in (2.5-cm), peeled and cut into thin strips
4 fresh green chili peppers, slit open lengthwise
½ teaspoon ground turmeric
2 cups (500 ml) coconut milk
2 teaspoons salt
4 red snapper fillets (about 6 oz/175 g each) or other firm white fish like cod or bass, skin on
1 teaspoon toasted and ground coriander seeds
1 teaspoon toasted and ground cumin seeds
½ teaspoon Asian red chili powder or cayenne pepper

For the sauce:

To make the sauce, heat 1 tablespoon of the oil in a large skillet over medium heat. Add the curry leaves, onions, ginger, and green chilies and cook, stirring until the onion is soft, about 5 minutes.

Add the turmeric, followed by the coconut milk and 1 teaspoon of salt and bring to a simmer. Cook for 3–5 minutes, until the sauce begins to turn glossy and thickens enough to coat the back of a spoon lightly. Set aside.

Heat the remaining oil in a large, heavy-bottomed skillet over high heat and add the snapper, skin-side down, and sear for about 1 minute per side, until golden brown. Move the pan off the heat. Sprinkle the remaining salt on both sides. Mix together the coriander, cumin, and the chili powder and sprinkle over the fish evenly. Place the pan back on heat and cook for another 30 seconds on each side. Serve with the coconut sauce.

Chapter 7 POULTRY AND MEAT

India owes its delectable cuisine to its rich heritage and culture. In fact, religion, along with key chapters in India's history, have played a big role in determining its cuisine and palette. For example, with the advent of the Mughals, and a country that was largely vegetarian slowly embraced meat and poultry over the course of nearly 200 years of Mughal rule. Military invasions and the country's key positioning on trade routes also helped shape some of today's more popular dishes. Vindaloo from the Portuguese as well as kebabs and pilaf (or *pulao*) from the Greeks and Persians are examples of such influences. Geography too had a role to play in giving Indian cuisine its regional variations. For inland populations, lamb, goat, and chicken started forming the basis of many popular dishes owing to the inaccessibility of fresh seafood, which only the coastal inhabitants had in abundance. Moreover, dishes from the south are spicier than those from the north, and their distinct flavor comes from the generous use of locally available tamarind, coconut, and mustard seeds.

Turkey is almost unused in India, owing to its unavailability. However, I have tried many of these recipes using turkey, and it works well. For those who prefer using leaner meat, you can substitute turkey for chicken in some of these recipes.

In India and on the subcontinent, lamb is rarely eaten in the average home, although you may find it in restaurants. We in the West are rather reluctant to eat mutton, in no small part because of its scarcity here. Traditionally, Indian meat recipes would generally call for goat, but feel free to substitute beef or lamb, per your preference.

There are hundreds of ways to prepare meat in the Indian style. You can mince it and mix with spices to make various kinds of kebabs and *kofta*s, use pieces in stews mixed with lentils, or just braise it with spices and serve with bread or rice. All the dishes in this chapter are treated as the main dish in a meal, with the side dishes (appetizers, vegetables, and accompaniments) planned around it.

Kerala-Style Chicken Stew

Use boneless country chicken for this recipe, as it gives this dish the best flavor. The traditional recipe from Kerala uses a paste of fresh coconut, green chili, ginger, onions, and turmeric, but here the recipe uses canned coconut milk for quick and easy preparation. Cook this warming stew when you need some comfort food. Serve it with hot over steamed rice.

Serves 4
Prep time: **15 minutes**
Cook time: **30 minutes**

10–12 (about 1 lb/500 g) small new or baby
   potatoes
Salt, to taste
¼ teaspoon ground turmeric
2 tablespoons oil
1 tablespoon ghee
½ teaspoon mustard seeds
1 cinnamon stick, ½-in (1.25-cm)
1 bay leaf
4 green cardamom pods
2 cloves peeled garlic, crushed, and sliced
   lengthwise
1 piece fresh ginger, 1-in (2.5-cm), peeled and
   thinly-sliced
20 curry leaves
1 teaspoon black peppercorn, crushed
2 onions (about ¾ lb/350 g), chopped
2 fresh green chili peppers, slit and crushed
1¼–1½ lbs (600–750 g) skinless, boneless
   chicken pieces cut into cubes, 2-in (5-cm)
1 carrot, peeled and diced (about ¾ cup/112 g)
Salt, to taste
3 cups (750 ml) coconut milk
½ cup (125 ml) water, if needed
½ cup (60 g) green peas, fresh or frozen
¼ teaspoon Café Spice Garam Masala (page 22)

Scrub the potatoes and parboil them in their skins with a pinch of salt and turmeric.

Heat the oil and ghee in a medium saucepan over medium heat and add the mustard seeds. When the seeds crackle, add the cinnamon, bay leaf, and cardamom. When the mixture turns fragrant, about 5–10 seconds, add the sliced garlic, sliced ginger (saving a little for a garnish), and curry leaves and continue to stir-fry. After 20 seconds, add the crushed peppercorns, onions, and green chili peppers and stir-fry for about 2–3 minutes. Add the chicken pieces and sauté for 2–3 minutes.

Add the parboiled potatoes and carrots. Salt to taste and cook, covered, for 2 minutes. Finally add the coconut milk, ½ cup (125 ml) of water (if needed), the green peas, and remaining thinly-sliced ginger. Sprinkle with the Garam Masala, cover, and cook until the chicken is fully cooked. Serve hot.

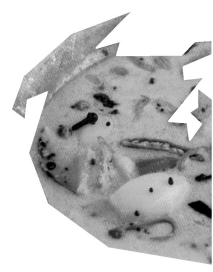

Omelet Curry Masala Anda

This recipe evokes fond memories of my aunt's kitchen back home. I remember that my young cousins were not particularly fond of eggs in their curry, so my aunt used this innovative method to add pieces of omelet instead—kids love omelet in a curry. You can use any filling in this omelet to give it your own twist. Play around with the masalas to create variations of this omelet curry.

Serves 2
Prep time: **15 minutes**
Cook time: **30 minutes**

2 tablespoons shredded unsweetened coconut (frozen or freshly grated)
½ teaspoon cumin seeds
½ teaspoon fennel seeds
1 tablespoon coriander seeds
½ teaspoon Asian red chili powder or cayenne pepper
¼ teaspoon ground turmeric
½ teaspoon Café Spice Garam Masala (page 22)
3 eggs
1 red onion, minced (about 1 cup/200 g)
2 fresh green chili peppers, seeded and finely chopped
2 tablespoons fresh coriander leaves (cilantro), chopped
Freshly ground black pepper, to taste
Salt, to taste
3 tablespoons oil
1 large onion (about 8 oz/250 g), sliced
2 fresh green chili peppers, chopped
2 tomatoes (about 1 lb/500 g), chopped
Juice of ½ lime
3 cups (750 ml) water
2 tablespoons minced fresh coriander leaves (cilantro)

Put the coconut, cumin and fennel seeds, coriander, red chili powder, turmeric, and Garam Masala into a blender with 2 tablespoons of water and grind to a paste. Set aside.

To make the omelet, whisk the eggs in a small bowl. Add the onion, green chilies, coriander leaves, and black pepper; salt to taste and mix well.

Heat 1 tablespoon of oil in a large nonstick pan or a skillet over medium heat. Add the egg and spread around to make a thin omelet.

When the lower side of the omelet is cooked, about 2–3 minutes, turn the omelet over gently using a large spatula. Once the other side is cooked, remove from the heat and cool.

Cut the omelet in half and then cut crosswise into strips, 1-in (2.5-cm) wide. Roll up the strips and set aside on paper towels.

To make the curry, heat the remaining oil in the medium nonstick skillet and fry the sliced onions over medium heat for 8–10 minutes until slightly brown. Add the ground spice paste and fry for another 3–4 minutes. Add a little water if the mixture sticks to the pan, but make sure the spices cook until fragrant.

Add the green chilies and tomatoes and sauté for 5 minutes. Then add the lime juice, water and salt to taste. Simmer for 10 minutes.

Add the coriander leaves and omelet strips. Cook for another 2 minutes over a very low heat until the sauce coats the omelet strips. Serve hot.

Mom's Chicken Curry Kori Ghassi

This is my family's recipe. It is one of my personal favorites for many reasons—including that it reminds me of my mother's home cooking and Sunday brunch back home. Sometimes I make this curry just for me when I am missing mom's food. I can never get enough of it. This dish is best served over rice or served with bread.

Serves 4
Prep time: **15 minutes**
Cook time: **30 minutes**

10 dried red chili peppers
1¼ cups (125 g) shredded unsweetened coconut (frozen or freshly grated)
1 teaspoon cumin seeds
2 teaspoons coriander seeds
1 teaspoon sesame seeds
3 cloves
6 peppercorns
1 cinnamon stick, ½-in (1.25-cm)
3 green cardamom pods
1 piece fresh ginger, 1-in (2.5-cm), peeled and chopped
1 tablespoon minced garlic
1 onion (about 5 oz/150 g), coarsely chopped
⅓ cup (80 ml) oil
1 whole chicken (about 2½–3½ lbs/1–1½ kg), cut into bone-in pieces
2 tomatoes (about ¾ lb/350 g), finely chopped
Salt, to taste
3 cups (750 ml) coconut milk
Juice of ½ lime
½ teaspoon Café Spice Garam Masala (page 22)

Soak the red chilies in a little water for 15–20 minutes to soften.

Place the cumin seeds, coriander seeds, sesame seeds, cloves, peppercorns, cinnamon, cardamom, ginger, garlic, onion, and the soaked red chilies into a food processor and blend to a smooth paste, adding a little water if necessary.

Heat the oil in a large, heavy-bottomed pan over medium heat. When hot, add the spice paste and cook, stirring constantly for about 5 minutes until fragrant.

Add the chicken pieces and fry them in the paste for about 5 minutes, until seared. Add the chopped tomatoes and salt and cook for about 5 minutes. Add the coconut milk and leave to simmer until the chicken is cooked, about 10–15 minutes. Add the lime juice and Garam Masala. Season with more salt if needed. Add more water if you need more gravy.

Chicken Tikka Masala
Murg Tikka Makhni

Chicken Tikka Masala, or "CTM," as it is popularly known these days, is the number one best seller at Café Spice. The CTM at Café Spice has a national popularity and has been a well-guarded secret all this time. For the benefit of the readers of this book, here is how you can get closest to the recipe! At Café Spice, the *makhni* gravy and the chicken are prepared separately. I have used an easier home version in this recipe that makes the CTM equally tasty.

Serves 4
Prep time: 15 minutes plus 2 hours for marinating
Cook time: 20 minutes

⅓ cup (80 ml) thick, Greek-style plain yogurt or sour cream
1 tablespoon plus 1 teaspoon paprika
2 teaspoons ground coriander
3 teaspoons Café Spice Garam Masala (page 22)
1 tablespoon plus 1 teaspoon Ginger-Garlic Paste (page 22)
1¼–1½ lbs (600–750 g) skinless, boneless chicken pieces cut into 2-in (5-cm) cube
Nonstick cooking spray or oil, to grease grill pan
2 tablespoons oil
1 large red onion (about 8 oz/250 g), minced
1¼ cups (300 ml) tomato purée
2½ tablespoons tomato paste
1 teaspoon salt, plus more if needed
4 tablespoons chopped fresh coriander leaves (cilantro)

2 tablespoons softened butter (optional)

Mix together 2 tablespoons of the yogurt or sour cream, 2 teaspoons of the paprika, 1 teaspoon of the ground coriander, 1 teaspoon of Café Spice Garam Masala, and half of the Ginger-Garlic Paste in a large mixing bowl. Add the cubed chicken and mix until the chicken pieces are well coated. Let marinate in the refrigerator for 2 hours.

Heat a grill pan over medium heat and grease with nonstick cooking spray or a little oil. Place the chicken cubes on the grill pan and cook all sides until well browned, about 4–5 minutes per side. Set aside.

Heat the oil in a large, heavy-bottomed skillet over medium-high heat. When hot, add the onion and sauté until translucent, about 1 minute. Add the remaining Ginger-Garlic Paste and cook until the mixture turns golden brown, about 1–2 minutes. Add the remaining paprika and ground coriander. Mix well and cook for another 30 seconds.

Add the tomato purée, tomato paste, and salt, and cook, stirring constantly, until the oil separates from the *masala*, about 2 minutes. This technique is called *bhunao*. Remove from the heat.

Transfer the onion-tomato mixture to a food processor or blender and process to a smooth paste. Add a little water if the mixture gets too thick.

Pour the tomato-onion purée back in the skillet and set over medium heat. Whisk in the remaining yogurt or sour cream, making sure it is well blended.

Add the chicken and reduce the heat to medium-low. Cover the pan and allow the chicken to simmer until it is completely cooked, about 7–8 minutes. Stir in the remaining Café Spice Garam Masala, the fresh coriander leaves, and butter, if using, and mix well. Taste for seasoning and add more salt if needed. Serve hot.

Tandoori Spiced Roasted Chicken   Murg Tandoori

Known as the "King of the Kebab," tandoori chicken is the best-known Indian delicacy and the tastiest way to barbecue chicken. The chicken should be marinated for at least four hours, but the longer you marinate the chicken, the better it tastes. The use of red food coloring, which creates the unique red color for which this dish is known, is optional. I've included instructions for roasting the chicken pieces in the oven or grilling them on a gas or charcoal grill, which will create a more authentic flavor.

Serves 4
Prep time: **20 minutes plus 4 hours for marinating**
Cook time: **30 minutes**

1 whole chicken, approximately 3½ to 4 lbs (1.6–
   1.75 kg), skinned, or 3½ to 4 lbs (1.6–1.75 kg)
   bone-in chicken pieces of your choice, skinned
1 teaspoon Asian red chili powder or cayenne
   pepper
1 teaspoon paprika
3 teaspoons salt
Juice of 1 lemon
4 tablespoons malt vinegar
⅓ cup (90 g) plain yogurt
½ cup (125 ml) heavy cream
1 piece fresh ginger, 2-in (5-cm), peeled and
   coarsely chopped
4 tablespoons coarsely chopped garlic
1 fresh green chili pepper, coarsely chopped
1 teaspoon ground cumin
1 teaspoon Café Spice Garam Masala (page 22)
1 teaspoon saffron threads
1 drop red food coloring (optional)
1 cup (2 sticks/225 g) melted butter, for basting
4 lime wedges
Mint Chutney (page 27), for serving

If using a whole chicken, cut the chicken into four
   parts, following the tip below.
Using a cleaver or a large chef's knife, cut the legs
   into two pieces (thigh and drumstick) and the
breasts into four pieces. If cutting the legs in two is too daunting, just leave them whole. Cut slits 2-in (5-cm) long, and deep enough to reach the bone, into each side in the leg pieces. Make similar slits on the breast pieces.

Mix together the Asian red chili powder or cayenne pepper, paprika, salt, lemon juice, and vinegar in a small bowl to make paste. Rub the paste over the chicken pieces evenly and into the slits. Set aside to marinate for 15–20 minutes.

Place the yogurt, cream, ginger, garlic, green chili pepper, cumin, Café Spice Garam Masala, saffron, and food coloring in a food processor or blender and process to make a smooth paste. Rub the chicken pieces with this yogurt mixture, making sure the marinade goes into the slits in the chicken. Let marinate in the refrigerator for at least 4 hours or overnight.

To roast the chicken: Preheat the oven to its highest setting. Take the chicken out of the marinade and place it on a rack in a rectangular baking pan or roaster. Roast the chicken for 25–30 minutes or until done. This technique is called *bhunnana*. Baste the chicken pieces with the melted butter during the roasting process. Serve garnished with lime wedges.

To grill the chicken: Set up the grill for cooking with two heat zones—high and medium—and preheat. (Note: The larger pieces of chicken will cook more slowly than the smaller ones. To have perfectly cooked chicken pieces that are all done at the same time, it is best to use two heat zones.) As the smaller pieces become cooked, move them to the low-heat side of the grill to keep them warm while the larger pieces continue to cook. If your grill doesn't have the capability to create multiple heat zones, simply put the large chicken pieces on first, followed by the smaller pieces. Cook the chicken pieces for about 10–15 minutes, then turn and cook the other side. Baste the chicken pieces with the melted butter during the grilling process. In about 25–30 minutes, the chicken should be cooked. As the chicken cooks, it becomes firmer. To judge doneness, look for good color and firmer meat on the bottom side of the chicken. To be completely sure of doneness, cook until the internal temperature reaches 165 F° (74°C).

TIPS FOR CUTTING WHOLE CHICKEN AND CHICKEN PIECES—There are different ways to quarter a whole chicken, but the easiest and fastest is to start with the legs. Take a leg in your hand and feel along it until you find the upper joint between the thighbone and leg. This feels like an indentation in the bone. Using a sharp, large knife, cut at the joint. The leg will separate from the breast with ease. Repeat with the other leg. Cut the chicken in half down the center, through the middle of the breast plate. You will now have 4 large pieces.
CUTTING BONE-IN CHICKEN PIECES—Cutting breasts, thighs, and legs into smaller segments isn't difficult. All you need is a large, sharp knife. Legs, owing to their thicker bone, cause a greater challenge and can be more easily cut with a sturdy cleaver. If cutting the legs in two is too daunting, simply leave them whole.

Curried Chicken Meatball **Kofta Murg Masala**

Use a smooth mince in this preparation to make the *kofta* (meatballs) smooth and full of flavor. This great, make-ahead recipe is perfect for a party or large crowd. Simple, easy, flavorful, and a crowd pleaser...you can't go wrong with this one! I use ground chicken for these spicy fragrant meatballs, but you can use any other meat like beef, turkey, or lamb. If you have leftovers from dinner, use them in a wrap with some veggies and lettuce for the next day's lunch.

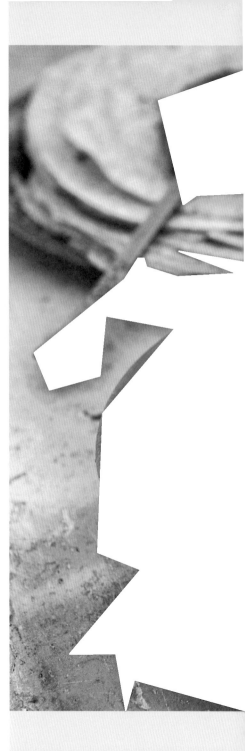

Serves 4
Prep time: **25 minutes**
Cook time: **30 minutes**

1½ lbs (750 g) ground chicken
1 bunch fresh coriander (cilantro) leaves and
    stalks (about 4 oz/125 g), chopped
2 onion (about 1.5 lbs/750 g), minced
¾ teaspoon Café Spice Garam Masala (page
    22)
2 tablespoons minced ginger
2 tablespoons minced garlic
1 large egg, whisked
½ cup (45 g) dried bread crumbs
½ teaspoon salt
3 tablespoons oil
½ teaspoon fennel seeds
2 bay leaves
1 cinnamon stick, ½-in (1.25-cm)
2 tomatoes (about ¾ lb/350 g), finely chopped
1 tablespoon tomato ketchup
3½ cups (875 ml) water
½ teaspoon ground turmeric
½ teaspoon Asian red chili powder or cayenne
    pepper
2 teaspoons ground coriander
Salt, to taste

Combine the ground chicken, half the coriander leaves and stalks, half the onions, Garam Masala, half the minced ginger and garlic, egg, bread crumbs, and salt in a large mixing bowl. Mix well using your hands.

Dip your hands in water and form about 30 meatballs, each about the size of a golf ball. Placed on a prepared tray, cover with plastic wrap, and place in the refrigerator for 15 minutes to chill.

Heat the oil in a large, deep nonstick saucepan over medium heat. Add the fennel seeds, bay leaves, cinnamon, and remaining chopped onion and cook, stirring often, until the onion is golden brown, about 5 minutes.

Add the finely chopped tomatoes and remaining ginger and garlic to the pan. Cook, stirring over a medium heat until the oil comes to the surface, about 7–8 minutes. Add 1 cup (250 ml) of the water and continue cooking until all the water has evaporated. Stir-fry this paste for about 3 minutes and then add the ground spices and salt. Add the remaining water, cover, bring to a boil and simmer for 5–6 minutes.

Add the meatballs to the pan, cover, and simmer for 15–20 minutes. Shake the pan every so often, but do not stir, as the meatballs could break. Add the remaining coriander leaves and stalks, stir the meatballs gently. Serve hot.

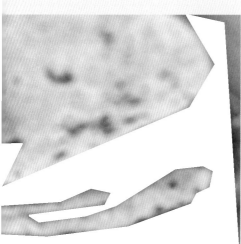

Easy Lamb Curry **Masala Gosht**

Lamb curry is an easy and flavorful dish that I usually make with bone-in loin chop. For this recipe however, I have called for a boneless leg of lamb to make it easier to eat. However, I do like a bone-in cut as the bones give extra flavor to the curry. This dish goes great with plain boiled or steamed rice. You may also serve this dish with any Indian breads such as Whole Wheat Griddle Bread (page 122) or Naan Bread (page 121). This version is quick and easy, and the addition of green chilies and coriander gives it extra zing.

Serves 6
Prep time: **15 minutes, plus 4 hours for marinating**
Cook time: **30 minutes**

½ cup (125 g) plain yogurt, whisked until smooth
4 tablespoons Ginger-Garlic Paste (page 22)
2 teaspoons Asian red chili powder or cayenne pepper
½ teaspoon ground turmeric
4 tablespoons chopped fresh coriander leaves (cilantro)
2½ lbs (1 kg) boneless leg of lamb, cut into cubes, 1-in (2.5-cm)
3 tablespoons oil
3 red onions (about 1 lb/500 g) chopped
6 green cardamom pods
4 cloves
3 tomatoes (about 1 lb/500 g), finely chopped
10–12 curry leaves
3 teaspoons salt
3–4 cups (750 ml–1 liter) warm water

Put the yogurt, Ginger-Garlic Paste, red chili powder, turmeric, and 2 tablespoons of coriander leaves in a large bowl. Mix well. Add the meat to this mixture and mix well. Cover with plastic wrap and marinate in the refrigerator for at least 2–4 hours or overnight.

Heat the oil in a large, nonstick saucepan over medium-high heat. Add the onions and cook, stirring until medium-brown, about 5–7 minutes. Add the cardamom pods and cloves and fry for 1 minute.

Add the meat with the marinade and cook for 8–10 minutes until the marinade is absorbed. Then sauté the meat, stirring continuously for about 5 minutes.

Add the tomatoes and cook for 5 minutes until the liquid is absorbed. Add the curry leaves and salt and warm water (depending on the consistency of gravy you require).

Reduce the heat to medium-low, cover, and simmer until the lamb is tender and the sauce is thick, about 20–25 minutes. Serve hot, garnished with the remaining chopped coriander leaves.

Lamb and Spinach Saagwala Gosht

Spinach and lamb make great winter comfort food. You can add homemade cottage cheese or paneer as well. I have used chopped spinach for texture and appearance in this recipe, instead of puréed spinach.

Serves 6
Prep time: 15 minutes, plus 4 hours for marinating
Cook time: 30 minutes

1 cup (250 g) plain yogurt, whisked to smooth
4 tablespoons Ginger-Garlic Paste (page 22)
2 fresh green chili peppers, minced
1 teaspoon Café Spice Garam Masala (page 22)
2½ lbs (1 kg) boneless leg of lamb, cut into cubes, 1-in (2.5-cm)
¼ cup (65 ml) oil
1 cinnamon stick, ½-in (1.25-cm)
2 bay leaves
12 black cardamom pods
3 cloves
2 onion (about 1.5 lb/750 g), minced
2 teaspoons ground coriander
1 teaspoon ground cumin
2¼ cups (565 ml) water
3 tomatoes (about 1 lb/500 g), finely chopped
1 tablespoon tomato paste
2 teaspoons salt
4 cups (200 g) packed fresh spinach leaves, washed and chopped or
    1½ cups (300 g) frozen chopped spinach, thawed
¼ teaspoon nutmeg powder
1 tablespoon unsalted butter (optional)

Place the yogurt, Ginger-Garlic Paste, green chili peppers, and Garam Masala in a large bowl and mix well. Add the meat to this mixture and mix well. Cover with plastic wrap and marinate in the refrigerator for at least 2–4 hours or overnight.

Heat the oil in a large saucepan over medium-high heat. Add the cinnamon, bay leaves, cardamom, and cloves and stir-fry until fragrant, about 10–15 seconds. Add the onion. Sauté for 15 minutes over low to moderate heat.

Add the ground coriander and cumin and sauté for 2 minutes, stirring continuously. Add ¼ cup (65 ml) of the water and cook for another 2 minutes to ensure that the spices are cooked.

Add the meat along with its marinade, stir well, and cook over moderate heat for 10 minutes until the yogurt is absorbed. Sauté the meat for 3 minutes, stirring continuously. Add the tomatoes and tomato paste and cook for another 2–3 minutes.

Add the remaining 2 cups (500 ml) of water and the salt. Turn the heat to low, cover with a lid, and leave to simmer for about 20–25 minutes until the lamb is tender. Add the chopped spinach and mix well. Cook for 5 minutes, uncovered.

When ready to serve, sprinkle with a little nutmeg powder and top with the butter, if using. Serve hot.

Lamb Shank Korma Nalli Gosht Korma

Although, there are a lot of steps and ingredients in this recipe, the end result is well worth the trouble, and it tastes even better the next day (like all good curries should). You can vary the amount of chilies you use in this dish to keep it in line with your preferred amount of spice! Also, although this recipe calls for lamb shanks, you could very well use better cuts of meat; and the better the cut (be it a chop or a steak), the better the taste will be.

Serves 4
Prep time: **15 minutes**
Cook time: **50 minutes**

1 teaspoon saffron threads
1 tablespoon rosewater
½ cup (125 ml) oil
3 onions (about 2½ lbs/1 kg), thinly sliced
1 cup (100 g) slivered almonds
4 fresh green chili peppers, chopped
1 cinnamon stick, ½-in (1.25-cm)
1 teaspoon cumin seeds
3 tablespoons Ginger-Garlic Paste (page 22)
4 lamb shanks, about 1 lb (500 g) each, trimmed of visible fat
2 teaspoons ground coriander
1 teaspoon Café Spice Garam Masala (page 22)
Salt, to taste
2 teaspoons Asian red chili powder or cayenne pepper
1 cup (230 g) thick, Greek-style plain yogurt or sour cream
4 cups (1 liter) water
¾ teaspoon ground mace
½ teaspoon ground cardamom
Juice of 1 lime

Soak the saffron strands in the rosewater for about 15–20 minutes.

Heat half the oil over medium-high heat in a large, thick-bottomed saucepan and stir-fry the onions until medium-brown. Add the almonds and continue to fry until the onions are deep brown, about 5–7 minutes.

Using a spatula, extract the oil from the onions by pressing them against the side of the pot. Transfer the onions and almonds to a blender and purée to a smooth paste.

Heat the remaining oil and sauté the green chili peppers, cinnamon, cumin seeds, and Ginger-Garlic Paste until fragrant, 2–3 minutes. Turn up the heat, add the lamb shanks, and sear on all sides for about 3 minutes. Add the ground coriander, ½ teaspoon Garam Masala, the red chili powder, and the yogurt. Stir continuously for 3 minutes and leave to simmer until the yogurt is absorbed, about 10 minutes.

Add the fried onion purée and mix well. Add the water and simmer until the meat is tender, about 45–60 minutes. Add the remaining Garam Masala, ground mace, and ground cardamom and mix well. Before transferring to a serving dish, stir in the lime juice and the saffron-rose water.

Dried Bombay Beef

This delicious dish is a favorite among most of my friends. It can be served not just as a beer-snack when friends visit, but also as a main course dish with *dosai*. If you manage to get coconut cooking oil and use it as the medium for frying the beef, it will impart the perfect authentic flavor of Indian coastal cooking. If you have any leftovers (which is unlikely!), use them with some lettuce in a wrap or in a taco the next day for lunch.

Serves 4
Prep time: **30 minutes plus at least 6–8 hours to marinate the beef**
Cook time: **30 minutes**

1¼ to 1½ lbs (600 g to 750 g) beef fillet, cut into very thin strips
1 teaspoon Asian red chili powder or cayenne pepper
1 teaspoon red chili flakes
1 piece of fresh ginger, 1-in (2.5-cm), peeled and grated
Salt, to taste
2 teaspoons freshly ground black pepper
2 teaspoons coconut oil (optional)
Oil, for deep-frying
1 red onion (about 5 oz/150 g), sliced
2 dried red chili peppers, broken in half
2 fresh green chili peppers, slit
1 teaspoon sugar
Juice of 2 limes
3 tablespoons rice flour

Mix the sliced beef with half the red chili powder, the chili flakes, ginger, salt, and pepper in a large bowl. Add the coconut oil, if using, and mix well. Let the meat marinate for 15–20 minutes before cooking.

Heat 1 tablespoon of the oil in a large skillet over medium-high heat and add the onion, red chili peppers, green chili peppers, remaining red chili powder, and a pinch of salt. Cook, stirring constantly, for 5–6 minutes until the onion is soft and translucent. Add the sugar and fry for a few more minutes until the onion begins to caramelize. Add the lime juice and take the pan off the heat.

Heat 2 inches (5 cm) of oil in a kadhai, small wok, or large saucepan over medium heat to 325°F (160°C) on a deep-fry or a candy thermometer. Toss the beef in the rice flour until evenly coated, then deep-fry in batches for 2–3 minutes until brown and crisp. Drain on a plate lined with paper towels. When all the beef has been cooked, toss the beef strips with the onion mixture and sliced chili. Transfer to a warm plate and serve immediately.

Pork Vindaloo

The term *vindaloo* derives from the Portuguese dish of meat, usually pork, prepared with vinegar and garlic. This curry is one of the many tasty, hot pork dishes originally from Goa, where the cooking style combines Portuguese influences, including the eating of pork, with fiery Indian flavors. What makes this dish unique is the combination of hot spices and vinegar. It tastes better if it is allowed to "pickle" for an entire day. Vindaloo is a popular dish in many parts of India. In the eastern states of Orissa and West Bengal, the same dish (not referred to as "vindaloo") is prepared for celebratory events as well as for home dinners, though it is hotter and contains more potato. I recommend that you ask your butcher to leave some fat from the skin on the meat, as it imparts a good flavor to the sauce. This dish is best when served with Brown Basmati Rice (page 119) or crusty French bread. Although this recipe uses pork, the Chicken Vindaloo from Café Spice is also very popular.

Serves 4
Prep time: 30 minutes plus at least 6–8 hours to marinate the pork
Cook time: 30 minutes

1½ lbs (750 g) leg or shoulder of pork, cut into cubes, 1-in (2.5-cm)
2 tablespoons malt vinegar
2 teaspoons freshly ground black pepper
1 teaspoon sugar
2 teaspoons Café Spice Garam Masala (page 22)
3 fresh green chili peppers, minced
1 teaspoon salt, plus more if needed
¼ cup (65 ml) oil
1 onion (about 5 oz/150 g), chopped
1 cup (500 g) Vindaloo Curry Paste
¼ cup (65 ml) tomato purée
4 cups (1 liter) water
1 large potato (about 10 oz/300 g), peeled and diced
4 tablespoons chopped fresh coriander leaves (cilantro)

VINDALOO CURRY PASTE

5 dried red chili peppers, crushed
1 teaspoon black peppercorns
1 teaspoon cumin seeds
1 teaspoon black mustard seeds
1 tablespoon peeled and minced fresh ginger
1 tablespoon minced garlic
½ teaspoon sugar
Salt, to taste
¼ cup (65 ml) white vinegar

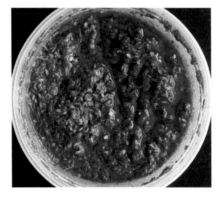

In a large mixing bowl, add the pork cubes, vinegar, black pepper, sugar, Garam Masala, green chili peppers, and salt. Let the pork marinate in the refrigerator for a minimum of 6 hours, preferably overnight.

Prepare the Vindaloo Curry Paste by blending all the ingredients into a paste in a blender. Set aside.

Heat the oil in a large, heavy-bottomed saucepan. Add the onion and sauté over medium heat until golden brown, about 5–6 minutes. Add the Vindaloo Curry Paste and tomato purée and sauté until the fat separates from the *masala*, about 2 minutes. Add some water to prevent sticking, if needed.

Add the pork along with the marinade. Cook, stirring constantly, over high heat for 2 minutes. Add the water and bring to a boil. Add the potato, cover, and reduce the heat to low. Simmer until the pork is tender and potato is cooked, about 25–30 minutes. Check for seasoning and add more salt, if needed. Stir in the chopped fresh coriander leaves and serve hot.

Chapter 8 BREADS, RICE AND GRAINS

Bread is a fundamental part of the dining culture of India. Indian breads differ greatly from each other in appearance, texture, and taste. Varieties include thin breads, which are large, flat, and round; the ever-popular *naan;* layered, flaky flatbreads; and puffed breads, which are fried in oil. All varieties of bread contain flour, water, and salt. Whole wheat flour is used for *chapati* and *poori*, while *paratha* are made with refined white flour along with some oil, a little milk, and sometimes, egg. If the typical Indian breads are not available, I encourage you to experiment with bread such as burger buns that you get at your bakery or local store.

Rice is considered sacred in India and plays a significant role in Indian ceremonies and festivals. Usually used to complement curries, lentils, and vegetables, rice is a staple in most households in India. However, there is also a large number of recipes in which rice is an important ingredient in its own right. Probably the most renowned is *Biryani,* where rice is cooked together with meat, fish, or vegetables. This dish is hearty enough to be considered the main dish and can be served just with a raita or salad. Another similar dish is pilau or pilaf—a rice dish cooked in a seasoned, spiced broth. Pilaf has many variations depending on the ingredients you chooses to add—be it meat and vegetables, just bits of cooked onion, or simply mixes of spices and saffron. The best variety of rice to use in savory dishes is basmati. It has a distinct aroma and flavor. In India, it is grown in the foothills of Himalayas and can be aged for up to fifteen years to mature its distinctive aroma and nutty flavor.

Dosai is another staple that is a popular choice for families from southern India. It has now become a versatile dish that dots tables around the world. You can make *dosai* just how you like it to please your taste buds. It can be just plain or filled with ingredients such as spiced potatoes, cheese, onions, carrots, or cashews. You can make it crispy or soft, thin or thick.

This chapter also includes a recipe using quinoa. Even though quinoa is often considered a whole grain, it is actually a seed that can be prepared like whole grains such as rice or barley. It is my favorite because it takes less time to cook, tastes great on its own, and has a higher protein content than any whole grain, which is perfect for vegetarians or vegans.

Coconut Rice Thengai Sadam

This rice dish is the result of a common but clever kitchen trick that is used in parts of southern India including Kerala, Karnataka, and Goa, where coconut is plentiful. Leftover rice is tossed with coconut and some spices to make a flavorful dish for the next day's lunch. Serve with seafood, meat, and chicken dishes. For best results, I recommend using freshly grated coconut.

Serves 4
Prep time: **10 minutes plus 40 minutes for soaking**
Cook time: **30 minutes**

2 cups (420 g) uncooked basmati rice
8 cups (2 liters) water
1 teaspoon salt
2 tablespoons ghee or oil
1 teaspoon mustard seeds
1 teaspoon cumin seeds
3 dried red chili peppers, whole
1 teaspoon split yellow peas (chana dal)
1 red onion (about 8 oz/250 g), thinly sliced
1 teaspoon minced fresh peeled ginger
Salt, to taste
1 cup (100 g) unsalted cashew nuts (optional)
8–10 curry leaves
1 cup (100 g) shredded unsweetened coconut (fresh or frozen)

Soak the rice for 30–40 minutes. Carefully pour out the soaking water and wash the rice in several changes of water until the water runs clear. Leave it to drain in a fine-meshed strainer for about 15 minutes.

Bring the water with the rice and salt to a boil in a heavy-bottomed saucepan. Lower the heat and simmer for 10–12 minutes, partially covered, until cooked. Drain the rice thoroughly in a fine-meshed strainer and return the rice to the saucepan. Set the pan aside, off the heat, covered.

Heat the ghee or oil in another heavy-bottomed saucepan over medium heat. Add the mustard seeds, cumin seeds, chili pepper, and split yellow peas and cook until fragrant, about 1–2 minutes. Add the onion and ginger and cook over moderate heat for another 4 minutes or until the onion is soft. Add the salt, cashew nuts (if using), curry leaves, coconut, and the cooked rice. Stir-fry over moderate heat until the rice is mixed in and all the flavors combined. Taste to check for seasoning and serve hot.

Lemon Rice with Peanuts Huli Anna

Lemon rice is a very popular everyday dish in southern India. It can be eaten hot, but tastes just as good at room temperature or cold alongside a spicy pickle (see Pumpkin Pickle, page 32). At Café Spice we dish out lemon rice with most of our mainstream entrees. In fact, our lemon rice recipe is as old as the company itself! The peanuts add an extra crunchy texture and sweetness to the rice.

Serves 4
Prep time: 10 minutes plus 40 minutes for soaking
Cook time: 15 minutes

2 cups (420 g) uncooked basmati rice
8 cups (2 liters) water
1 teaspoon ground turmeric
1 teaspoon salt
3 tablespoons oil
2 teaspoons black mustard seeds
3 dried red chili peppers
2 teaspoons split yellow peas (chana dal)
6–8 fresh curry leaves
1 cup (100 g) unsalted peanuts
Juice of 2 lemons, plus more if needed
Salt, to taste
Lemon wedges, for serving

Soak the rice for 30–40 minutes. Carefully pour out the soaking water and wash the rice in several changes of water until the water runs clear. Leave it to drain in a fine-meshed strainer for about 15 minutes.

Bring the water with the turmeric, rice, and salt to a boil in a heavy-bottomed saucepan. Lower the heat and simmer for 10–12 minutes, partially covered, until cooked. Drain the rice thoroughly in a fine-meshed strainer and return the rice to the saucepan. Set the pan aside, off the heat, covered.

Heat the oil in a small skillet over medium heat. Add the mustard seeds and when they start to pop, add the dried red chili peppers, split yellow peas, curry leaves, and peanuts. Cook, stirring constantly, for a minute or until the peas and the nuts are lightly browned. This technique is known as tempering.

Pour the contents of the skillet into a mixing bowl. Add the rice, lemon juice, and salt and mix until well combined. Taste for lemon and salt and adjust according to taste. Serve with lemon wedges.

Tomato and Curry Leaf Quinoa

Small, round, and a good source of protein, iron, and fiber, quinoa is a quick and flavorful way to get in a serving of wholesome nutrition. About the same size of couscous granules, quinoa cooks in about 10–15 minutes. The only special handling required is giving it a good rinse before cooking; otherwise it can leave a bitter aftertaste. Actually a seed, but prepared like a grain, quinoa is not found in India, but is indigenous to the Andean region of Peru, Ecuador, Bolivia, and Columbia. Quinoa is becoming very popular with weight watchers in the West. Here is my recipe for infusing it with the tantalizing, Indian flavor of curry leaves to give it an innovative twist.

Serves 2
Prep time: **10 minutes plus 15 minutes for soaking**
Cook time: **30 minutes**

⅔ cup (100 g) quinoa
2 cups (500 ml) water
Pinch of salt
2 tablespoons ghee or oil
1 dried red chili pepper, broken into pieces
1 teaspoon mustard seeds
10 fresh curry leaves
1 red onion (about 8 oz/250 g), chopped
1 fresh green chili pepper, chopped
1 piece fresh ginger, ½-in (1.25-cm), peeled and finely chopped
1 tomato (about 3½ oz/100 g), chopped
1½ teaspoons salt
¼ teaspoon Asian red chili powder or cayenne pepper
½ teaspoon sugar
2 tablespoons finely chopped fresh coriander leaves (cilantro)
Juice of ½ lemon

Soak the quinoa in cold water for 15 minutes, then drain and rinse. Bring the water with the salt to a boil in a medium saucepan. Add the rinsed quinoa and simmer for about 15 minutes until it is cooked but still retains some bite (quinoa develops a white ring round the circumference of each grain when it is about ready). Drain off any excess water.

Heat the ghee or oil in a heavy-bottomed saucepan and add the red chili pepper and mustard seeds. Let them crackle and splutter for about 10–15 seconds. Add the curry leaves and the onion and cook, stirring often, for 6–8 minutes until the onions turn golden brown.

Add the green chili pepper and ginger and cook, stirring for a minute. Add the chopped tomato, salt, red chili powder, and sugar and cook over medium heat for 8–10 minutes until most of the moisture from the tomato has evaporated and the mixture begins to come together.

Add the cooked quinoa and mix gently until heated through. Add the chopped coriander leaves and lemon juice. Mix thoroughly and serve hot.

Wild Mushroom and Spinach Rice Gucchi Palak Pulao

Usually in Indian cooking we will not use wild mushrooms like shiitake or morels. This is my adventurous creation, marrying a Western ingredient with Indian flavors. If you use dried mushrooms, soak in just-boiled water for twenty minutes, then drain the water. Perking up a regular rice dish with wild mushrooms like morels, shiitake, and oyster plus herbs, spices, and the added color from the spinach makes a great mid-week meal.

Serves 4
Prep time: **10 minutes plus 40 minutes for soaking**
Cook time: **20 minutes**

1½ cups (315 g) uncooked basmati rice
½ lb (250 g) fresh wild mushrooms such as chanterelle, morel, oyster, and shiitake
3 tablespoons oil
1 teaspoon cumin seeds
½ teaspoon fennel seeds
2 bay leaves
1 cinnamon stick, 1-in (2.5-cm)
5 green cardamom pods
5 black peppercorns
2 cloves
1 red onion (about 8 oz/250 g), peeled and chopped
1 cup (100 g) slivered almonds
2 cups (100 g) packed fresh spinach leaves, washed and chopped
1 tablespoon chopped garlic
Salt, to taste
2 cups (500 ml) water
1 teaspoon fresh lemon juice

Soak the rice for 30–40 minutes. Carefully pour out the soaking water and wash the rice in several changes of water until the water runs clear. Leave it to drain in a fine-meshed strainer for about 15 minutes.

Wipe and clean the mushrooms with damp paper towels. Cut any large mushrooms into slices.

Heat the oil in a large, wide saucepan. Add the whole spices (cumin, fennel, bay leaves, cinnamon, cardamom, black peppercorns, and cloves) and cook for 10–15 seconds or until fragrant. Add the diced onions and slivered almonds. Cook, stirring often, for about 4–5 minutes until the onions are soft and browning at the edges. Add the mushrooms, spinach, garlic, and salt and cook over a high heat for another 2–3 minutes.

Add the drained rice to the pan with the water, bring to a good boil, then cover with a lid, lower the heat, and cook until the water has evaporated, about 10 minutes. Take off the heat, remove the lid, and allow any excess moisture to evaporate. Gently stir in the lemon juice and taste and adjust the seasoning, if necessary.

Brown Basmati Rice

Brown basmati is becoming very popular in the West these days because of its nutritional benefits. It takes a little more time to cook than regular basmati, so be careful not to undercook it. Because this is unprocessed rice, I don't recommend it for everyday meals. You can use cumin and other spices to flavor this rice dish. Quick tip: Stir the rice and turn it over gently after the water has been absorbed to ensure that the grains are evenly cooked. By resting the cooked rice for fifteen minutes, you give the grains ample time to gain volume so that they don't stick to each other.

Serves 4
Prep time: 10 minutes plus 40 minutes for
   soaking
Cook time: 30 minutes

2½ cups (500 g) uncooked brown basmati
   rice
3 tablespoons ghee or oil
1 teaspoon cumin seeds
1 bay leaf
1 cinnamon stick, 1-in (2.5-cm)
4 green cardamom pods
1 red onion (about 8 oz/250 g), thinly sliced
5 cups (1.2 liters) water
2 tablespoons chopped fresh mint leaves
Salt, to taste

Soak the rice for 30–40 minutes. Carefully pour out the soaking water and wash the rice in several changes of water until the water runs clear. Leave it to drain in a fine-meshed strainer for about 15 minutes.

Heat the ghee or oil in a heavy-bottomed saucepan over medium heat. Add the cumin seeds, bay leaf, cinnamon, and cardamom pods. When they crackle, add the sliced onion and sauté until light golden brown. Add the drained rice to the pan and cook for another 2–3 minutes, taking care that the rice does not break.

Add the water, mint, and salt and bring to a boil. Reduce the heat to low, cover, and cook for about 20 minutes until the rice is tender and the water has been absorbed. Remove from the heat and stir the rice gently to mix. Cover the pan and leave to rest for 15–20 minutes before serving.

Simple Rice Pilaf Saada Pulao

This is a very simple way to turn an everyday rice dish into something exciting and flavorful. The flavor of roasted spices marries very well with any vegetable or meat dish, making this rice most convenient for any Indian menu fare. You can even make this dish with a single spice like the cumin or the peppercorns instead of using the entire array of combined spices.

Serves 4
Prep time: 5 minutes plus 40 minutes for soaking
Cook time: 15 minutes

1½ cups (315 g) uncooked basmati rice
1½ teaspoons cumin seeds
1 teaspoon whole cloves
½ teaspoon black peppercorns
5–7 green cardamom pods
1 tablespoon ghee (clarified butter) or oil
2¾ cups (685 ml) water
1 teaspoon salt
1 tablespoon chopped mint leaves

Soak the rice for 30–40 minutes. Carefully pour out the soaking water and wash the rice in several changes of water until the water runs clear. Leave it to drain in a fine-meshed strainer for about 15 minutes.
Place the cumin, cloves, black peppercorns, and cardamom in a medium saucepan and roast, while shaking the pan over medium-high heat until highly fragrant, about 1 minute. Add the drained rice and ghee or oil and sauté for 1–3 minutes, stirring gently with a wooden spoon—being careful not to break the grains of the rice.
Add the water and salt and bring to a boil over high heat. Reduce the heat to the lowest setting, cover the pan, and cook until the rice is done, 10–12 minutes. Do not stir the rice while it cooks. Remove from the heat and let the rice rest, covered, for 5 minutes. Transfer to a serving platter, garnish with the fresh mint, and serve.

Naan Bread

This bread is by far the most popular variety served in Indian restaurants. Traditionally, naan cooks against the superheated clay wall of a cylindrical tandoor. Heat radiating from the coals below also chars the exposed side, so the bread never needs to be flipped. My challenge for the longest time in my test kitchen was to find the right heat to replicate a tandoor. I initially thought that a grill or preheated pizza stone would best approximate the intense temperature of a tandoor, which cooks naan mainly by heat conducted through its walls. I discovered that there is a better alternative. Try the trusty, heavy-duty, cast-iron skillet. A covered skillet delivers heat to the bottom and top of the bread, producing naan that are nicely charred but still moist. To maintain the soft interior of the naan, spray the dough with water before cooking.

Makes 5
Prep time: **15 minutes plus 1 hour for resting**
Cook time: **15–20 minutes**

1¾ cups (225 g) all-purpose flour
2 teaspoons sugar
½ teaspoon salt
½ teaspoon baking powder
½ cup (125 ml, or a little extra) milk, warmed (about 110˚F/43˚C)
1 large egg yolk (optional)
2 tablespoons vegetable oil
Toppings (optional)—nigella seeds, poppy seeds, sesame seeds, chopped garlic, and fresh coriander leaves (cilantro) or chopped mint
1 tablespoon butter, melted for brushing

Sift together the flour, sugar, salt, and baking powder in a large mixing bowl. Whisk together the milk, yolk, and oil in a small bowl. Make a well in the center of the dry ingredients and pour in the liquids.

Slowly mix together the dough by working outward from the center and incorporating the flour from the edges of the well to make smooth, soft dough. Knead well for 8–10 minutes, adding a little flour if the dough is too sticky.

Place in an oiled bowl, cover with a damp dish towel, and leave for at least 1 hour in a warm place to rise.

Punch down the dough, knead it briefly, and divide it into 5 portions. Shape each piece into a smooth, tight ball. Place dough balls at least 2 inches (5 cm) apart on a lightly oiled baking sheet. Cover loosely with plastic wrap that has been coated with vegetable oil spray. Let stand for 15–20 minutes.

Adjust oven rack to middle position and heat oven to 400ºF (200ºC). Place a serving plate on the rack so that you can put the finished naan on it to keep them warm while the rest are cooking.

Transfer 1 ball to a lightly floured work surface and sprinkle with flour. Using hands and rolling pin, press and roll the piece of dough into 8-in (20-cm) oval or teardrop shape of even thickness, sprinkling the dough and work surface with flour as needed to prevent sticking. Then gently prick all over with a fork. Sprinkle on the seeds and/or toppings (if using) and press them into the dough.

Heat 1 teaspoon oil in a 12-in (30-cm) cast-iron skillet over medium heat until the oil shimmers. Wipe the oil out of the skillet completely with paper towels. Spray and mist top of dough lightly with water. Place dough in the pan, moistened side down. Mist the top surface of dough with water and cover. Cook until bottom is browned in spots across the surface, 2–4 minutes. Flip the naan, cover, and continue to cook on second side until lightly browned, 2–3 minutes. (Note—If the bread puffs up, gently poke with a fork to deflate.) Flip the naan, brush the top with about 1 teaspoon melted butter, transfer to the plate in the oven, and cover the plate tightly with aluminum foil. Repeat rolling and cooking the remaining 4 dough balls. Once the last naan is baked, serve hot.

VARIATION: ROYAL NAAN—To make this exquisite, special-occasion stuffed naan, pulse together ½ cup (75 g) unsalted pistachios, ¼ cup (30 g) raisins, and 1½ teaspoons sugar to make a coarse powder. Divide into five portions. Roll the naan into thick circles, fill each with one portion of the filling and pinch the dough around it to close. Roll out the naan again into teardrop or oval shapes. Sprinkle with ½ cup (50 g) slivered almonds and then cook and serve as mentioned above.

Whole Wheat Griddle Bread
Chapati

This is a staple accompaniment to most Indian dishes. To give it an interesting variation, you could use any spice or chopped up greens to flavor the chapati. Dunk it with any vegetable or gravy dish, with a side of a pickle, and you can have a flavorful, wholesome meal right there.

Makes about **10** *chapati*
Prep time: **10 minutes plus 1 hour for resting**
Cook time: **10 minutes**

2 cups (250 g) whole wheat flour, plus extra to dust work
    surface
½ teaspoon salt
About 1 cup (250 ml) water
½ cup (125 ml) oil or melted ghee (clarified butter), for
    brushing

REHEATING TIPS—Though chapati are best eaten hot off the griddle, they can also be refrigerated or frozen for later use. They can be kept in the refrigerator for up to 5–6 days and frozen for as long as 2 months. To store the breads, make sure the they are first cooled completely. Then stack them one on top of the other and tightly wrap in plastic wrap. Then wrap them with aluminum foil or place them in freezer bags. They can be reheated, wrapped in aluminum foil, in a 450ºF (230ºC) toaster oven; on a hot tava, griddle or skillet; under the broiler; or in a single layer on an ungreased broiler-safe tray, 4–5 in (10–12 cm) from the heat source.

Sift the whole wheat flour and salt into a bowl. Make a well in the center. Slowly add the water in small quantities, while mixing, until a soft dough is formed. Turn onto a floured work surface and knead the dough by pressing your knuckles lightly into the dough, spreading it outward, gathering the ends toward the center with your fingers, and pressing the center down. Repeat for about 3–5 minutes, or until you have soft, pliable dough that does not stick to your fingers.

Place the dough in an oiled bowl, cover with a damp cloth or plastic wrap, and let rest for about an hour. (This allows the gluten to develop). If keeping for longer periods, refrigerate the dough.

Heat a tava, griddle, or a large cast-iron skillet over medium heat. Divide the dough into 8–10 equal portions. Work with one portion at a time, keeping the rest covered with a damp cloth. On a lightly floured surface, roll out each portion into a circle about 6–7 in (15–18 cm) in diameter. Carefully shake off the excess surface flour prior to cooking.

Place each rolled bread on the tava, griddle, or skillet and cook for about 7–10 seconds, until brown. Turn the bread over to brown the other side, about 12–15 seconds. Turn it over and lightly smear the hot bread with the oil or ghee. Serve hot.

Semolina and Whole Wheat Dosai with Spiced Potatoes Rawa Masala Dosai

What *chapati* is for northern India, *dosai* (a rice and lentil crepe) is for the southern part of India. When we opened up Dosateria (our new, Indian crepe concept restaurant) in 2012, these semolina crepes became an instant hit. Here, I have called for adding semolina and whole wheat flour to the grist, but you can use only rice flour instead, if you wish. To make it from scratch using the original version involves a long, drawn-out process that might prove onerous, but this timesaving method using buttermilk is much simpler. The basic and traditional version, filled with spiced potatoes, can be served along with South Indian Lentils and Vegetables (page 56) to make a perfect meal.

Makes 12–15 *dosai*
Prep time: **15 minutes plus 30 minutes for resting**
Cook time: **30 minutes**

1 cup (150 g) medium-grain semolina
½ cup (65 g) rice flour
3 tablespoons whole wheat flour
½ cup (125 ml) buttermilk
1–1½ cups (250–375 ml) water (use as needed)
Salt, to taste
½ cup (20 g) fresh coriander leaves (cilantro), chopped
2 tablespoons shredded unsweetened coconut (freshly grated or frozen)
1 fresh green chili pepper, minced
½ teaspoon cumin seeds, toasted
2 medium potatoes, about 1 lb (500 g)
3 tablespoons oil
1 teaspoon mustard seeds
1 teaspoon split yellow peas (chana dal)
5–7 fresh curry leaves
1 red onion (about 4 oz/125 g), sliced
¼ teaspoon turmeric
½ teaspoon salt
½ cup (125 ml) clarified butter

To make the batter—Mix together the semolina, rice flour, whole grain flour, buttermilk, 1 cup (250 ml) of water, and salt in a medium bowl. Set aside until the semolina absorbs all the water, about 30 minutes.

Mix in the coriander, coconut, green chili pepper, and cumin seeds and whisk for a few seconds, adding enough of the remaining water to make a thin batter of pouring consistency (slightly thinner than pancake batter). If the batter becomes too thin, mix in some rice flour.

To make the potato filling—Combine the potatoes with enough cold water to cover them in a medium saucepan, bring to a boil over high heat, and cook uncovered, until very tender.

Drain the potatoes well and set aside to cool. Peel the potatoes and chop coarsely.

Heat the oil in a nonstick skillet over medium heat, add the mustard seeds, and let them pop. Add the split yellow peas, curry leaves, and sliced onion and fry for 1 minute. Stir in the turmeric and cook for another 30 seconds. Add the potatoes and cook over low heat for 5 minutes. Season with salt to taste and cool.

To assemble the dosai—Heat a nonstick skillet over medium heat. Lightly brush the surface of the pan with the clarified butter. Stir the batter and pour a ladleful into the middle of the pan and quickly spread it out with the back of the ladle to form a thin pancake. Drizzle the clarified butter around the edge to crisp up the pancake.

Cook until small holes appear on the surface and the edges start to brown. Turn over and cook until brown (optional). Serve hot with a scoop of potato filling in the center or on the side.

Fried Puffed Bread Poori

Deep-fried breads cannot be an everyday food, but these Indian breads are great for special occasions. You can add quickly prepared ingredients like chopped herbs to lend color and flavor to this dish. I like to serve this bread with a portion of Chickpea Curry with Sweet Potato (page 54), the way it is served in the streets in India. It is a very popular breakfast food in India. Get your kids to stand and watch the bread puff up while being fried—it's a lot of fun!

Makes 16 *poori*
Prep time: **10 minutes plus 30 minutes for resting the dough**
Cook time: **15 minutes**

1 cup (120 g) whole wheat flour
1 cup (120 g) all-purpose flour, plus extra to dust work surface
½ teaspoon salt
3 tablespoons oil
6–8 tablespoons water
Oil, for deep-frying

Sift both the flours in a bowl. Mix in the salt. Drizzle the oil into the flour mixture and rub it in with your fingers. Slowly add the water to form a medium-soft ball of dough. Turn onto a floured work surface and knead the dough by pressing your knuckles lightly into the dough, spreading the dough outward, gathering the ends toward the center with your fingers, and pressing the center down. Repeat for about 3–5 minutes or until you have soft, pliable dough that does not stick to your fingers. Form a smooth ball, rub it with a little oil, and place it in a mixing bowl covered with a plastic wrap. Set aside for 15–30 minutes.

Heat 2 inches (5 cm) of oil in a kadhai, small wok, or large saucepan over medium heat to 325°F (160°C) on a deep-fry or candy thermometer. To gauge the temperature of the oil without a thermometer, drop a piece of bread about 1-in (2.5-cm) square into the oil, turning it often as the oil heats up. When the oil reaches 325°F (160°C), the bread will begin to brown quickly and turn golden brown all over—like a crouton—in about 40 seconds.

As the oil heats up, divide the dough into 12 balls. Roll each ball into a 5-in (12.5 cm) circle. Keep the rolled poori covered with plastic wrap until ready to fry. When the oil is hot, carefully lay each poori on the hot oil without letting it fold up. It should sizzle immediately. Using the back of a slotted spoon, gently push the poori into the oil with quick strokes. It should puff up in seconds. Turn the poori over and cook for a few seconds, until slightly brown. Drain on paper towels. Serve immediately.

Chapter 9   DESSERTS AND DRINKS

Desserts, called *mithai* (sweets), have always been an integral part of Indian cuisine, with milk-based desserts being a predominant feature. An astounding variety of sweets is available from different parts of the country. While a whole serving may be a little too sweet for Western palates, a small portion of one of these exquisite desserts is the perfect ending to a meal.

Many Indian desserts are made with fruit, nuts, spices, and milk. Coconut is a natural ingredient for many sweet dishes in the southern and coastal parts of the country. Desserts are normally consumed after spicy meals, and some of them even contain ingredients like cardamom and saffron that often aid digestion. Indian desserts are very often decorated with cardamom seeds, raisins, almonds, pistachios, cashew nuts, and fruit such as mangoes, guava, pineapple, melon, red cherries, oranges, and bananas. In eastern India, where milk is ubiquitous, most sweets are made using milk and milk products.

Indian beverages are a popular part of the cuisine. The array includes drinks that are both unique and refreshing. Indian beverages, often referred to as "sherbets," are non-alcoholic and specifically formulated to beat the heat of the sultry Indian summer. Try the Tamarind Cooler (page 136), Chilled Mango Lassi (page 133), or Tender Coconut Cooler (page 136) to cool off on a hot day.

Tea, also known as "chai," is the most common form of drink in India, especially in the north. As winters there are extreme, warming tea is available anywhere one goes. Tea can be prepared in many ways, including spiced tea, "masala chai," and ginger tea. Coffee is a popular drink commonly consumed in the southern states of India.

The recipes in this chapter have been adapted from traditional Indian fare to focus on simplicity; nobody wants to wait for dessert!

Creamy Rice Pudding
Kheer

This creamy, cardamom-spiced rice pudding, known as *kheer*, can be enjoyed hot or cold and is probably the most popular pudding in India. It is often served during Indian festivals. When I was growing up, my mother would make it for the occasional, elaborate Sunday meal. The whole milk and cream can be replaced with nonfat milk for a lighter version. I have used basmati rice as I feel it makes the most flavorful Indian rice pudding. Kheer made with basmati is a northern Indian or a Punjabi specialty. In the south, they make a similar version using long-grain white rice and, in Bengal, they use Bengali short-grain rice. I've included a favorite twist on the traditional kheer using fresh, ripe mangoes. When making cardamom mango kheer, I like to use sweet mangoes like Champagne or Alphonso.

Serves 4
Prep time: **10 minutes plus 2 hours for cooling**
Cook time: **40 minutes**

⅓ cup (70 g) uncooked basmati rice
5½ cups (1.3 liters) whole milk
½ teaspoon ground cardamom
2 cups (500 ml) heavy cream, plus more if needed
⅓ cup (55 g) golden raisins
¼ cup (50 g) sugar
1 tablespoon slivered almonds, toasted, for garnish

Combine the rice and milk in a heavy-bottomed saucepan. Bring the milk to a gentle boil over medium-high heat. Once the milk has come to a boil, lower the heat and gently simmer for 35–40 minutes, uncovered, until most of the milk has been absorbed. Stir frequently while the rice is cooking to avoid scalding, which would add a burnt flavor to the pudding. (If you think the milk is beginning to burn, lower the heat and avoid scraping the bottom of pan.) Stir in the ground cardamom, cream, and golden raisins.

Remove from the heat and stir in the sugar. Let cool, stirring occasionally to prevent a skin from forming. This pudding will be thick and creamy. Stir in additional cream if the pudding is too thick. Refrigerate until cold. Serve in individual serving bowls, garnished with the toasted slivered almonds.

VARIATION: CARDAMOM MANGO KHEER—Peel and dice 2 ripe and sweet mangoes. Purée one of them using a blender. Add a pinch of ground cardamom and sugar to taste. Fold the mango purée into the cooked and cooled kheer. Use the rest as a topping.

Milk Dumplings in Saffron Syrup Gulab Jamoon

The closest resemblance to this dumpling here in the West, is the donut hole (Munchkin) that you can find at any Dunkin' Donuts location. Let's just say this is an Indian version! This recipe uses milk or milk powder instead of flour. It is made fragrant by the addition of the rosewater and saffron that are infused in the sugar syrup. The saffron also provides a beautiful golden color to the syrup. This dessert is widely enjoyed in India during festivals. It is best eaten warm, but it's also delicious when served cold. It is very important to soak the dumplings in the syrup before you serve them, or else they might be hard and dry. You can even be adventurous when making it for an extra-special occasion and add interesting stuffing, like a dry fruit or a chocolate morsel, inside the dumpling.

Serves 4–6
Prep time: **10 minutes plus 2 hours for cooling**
Cook time: **30 minutes**

⅔ cup (150 g) dried milk powder
⅓ cup (75 g) all-purpose flour
½ teaspoon baking soda
2 tablespoons unsalted butter, melted
2–4 tablespoons whole milk
Oil, for deep-frying

SAFFRON SYRUP
1½ cups (300 g) super fine sugar
1 cup (250 ml) water
2 tablespoons rosewater
A few strands of saffron

To prepare the Saffron Syrup, slowly dissolve the sugar and water in a saucepan over medium heat, then bring to a boil. Reduce the heat and simmer gently for 10 minutes until reduced and slightly thickened. Stir in the rosewater and saffron and remove from the heat and let cool.

In a large mixing bowl add the milk powder, flour, and baking soda and stir to combine. Make a well in the center, add the butter, and stir in enough milk to bring the ingredients together to form a stiff dough. Let the dough rest for 20 minutes.

Divide the dough into 18–20 pieces and gently roll each piece in your hands to form a smooth ball. (Do not roll the balls too firmly as you want them to have a soft and light texture when cooked.) Place the balls on a large plate and cover with a damp tea towel.

Heat the oil in a deep, wide saucepan over a medium heat. Keep the heat at a constant medium to low temperature, about 230º–260ºF (110º–130ºC). Deep-fry the milk balls in batches, adding them gently one at a time. These milk dumplings will sink at the bottom of the pan. It is very important to keep turning them to ensure a deep golden brown color all over. After about 3–4 minutes, they will rise to the surface. Continue to cook them slowly for another 2 minutes or until even golden brown.

Carefully remove the dumplings from the oil and drain on a plate lined with paper towels. Transfer the dumplings into the slightly warm Saffron Syrup. Ideally, let the dumplings sit in the Saffron Syrup overnight to soak and warm through gently before serving.

Coconut Fudge   Nariyal ki Burfi

Fudges in India are known as *burfi*, and there is usually an elaborate process that is followed to make them. Typically prepared for festive occasions in India—for example, during Diwal, the festival of lights—fudge is made in batches and boxed in colorful cartons to be given as gifts to family and friends. This recipe is simplified, but the end result definitely doesn't compromise on taste or the experience of eating a burfi! The combination of the coconut and cardamom makes this sweet a treat for the taste buds. I often use edible gold leaf to garnish these sweets because of the festive look it creates. You can purchase this flashy edible accoutrement from any French pastry shop.

Serves 4–6
Prep time: **15 minutes**
Cook time: **25 minutes**

2½ cups (250 g) shredded unsweetened coconut (freshly grated or frozen)
1 cup (100 g) desiccated coconut
½ cup (100 g) sugar
1 can condensed milk, 14-oz (400-g)
1 tablespoon ground cardamom, preferably freshly ground green cardamom seeds (from about 10 cardamom pods)
1 cup (2 sticks/200 g) unsalted butter, plus extra to grease
1 cup (110 g) roasted unsalted pistachios, finely chopped (optional)

Heat a medium, wide-mouthed pan over medium to low heat. Add the fresh coconut, desiccated coconut, sugar, and condensed milk. Cook stirring frequently for 20–25 minutes until the mixture has thickened to a fudge. Note—do not leave the pan unattended as the coconut mixture should not take on any brown, cooked color. Stir in the ground cardamom and butter and remove the pan from the heat.

Pour the coconut mixture into a lightly buttered baking dish and spread out to about 1–2 in (2–5 cm) thickness.

Top it with the pistachios (if using) and press them gently with the back of a spoon to help the nuts stick. Let the fudge cool completely, then chill for at least 30 minutes to allow it to firm up.

Cut the coconut fudge into small diamonds or squares. Serve at room temperature.

Chilled Mango Cooler Aam Panna

This Indian drink is renowned for its heat-dissipating properties. It is made from green mangoes and it is used as a tasty and healthy beverage to fight the intense heat of Indian summers. Apart from being tasty, this drink also looks good owing to its refreshing, light green color. The drink is welcome on a hot day, and after a meal it's great as a digestive.

Serves 4
Prep time: **20 minutes**
Cook time: **15 minutes**

3 green mangoes (1¼ lbs/600 g total), peeled and diced
4 cups (1 liter) water
Salt, to taste
¼ cup (10 g) packed fresh mint leaves

¼ cup (50 g) sugar
½ teaspoon cumin seeds, toasted and ground
Crushed ice, for serving
Mint sprigs, for serving

Put the diced mangoes, with enough water to cover, in a medium saucepan over medium heat. Cook the raw mangoes until slightly tender, about 10–15 minutes. Drain and cool.

Blend the cooked mangoes with the water, salt, and mint leaves. Strain the mixture in a sieve.

Add the sugar and roasted cumin powder to the mango mixture. Mix well and chill.

Add the crushed ice into four tall 8-oz (250-ml) glasses and pour in the drink. Serve garnished with the mint sprigs.

Lassi

Lassi is an ever-popular Indian drink. Here I have used plain yogurt. You can use vanilla-flavored yogurt for a slightly different taste. You can use fresh mangoes, or if using pulp, use Alphonso and Kesar mango pulp.

Serves 4

Prep time: 5 minutes if using canned mango purée, 15 minutes if using fresh mangoes

4 cups (1 kg) plain yogurt
2 tablespoons sugar, or to taste
3 ripe mangoes (about 3 lbs/1.5 kg), peeled and cut into chunks, or 3 cups (750 ml) canned mango pulp or purée
½ teaspoon ground cardamom, preferably freshly ground green cardamom seeds (from about 6 green cardamom pods)
1 cup (250 ml) crushed ice

Blend all the ingredients in an electric blender until the yogurt is frothy. Pour into four 8-oz (250-ml) glasses and serve.

VARIATION: CUCUMBER LASSI— Compared to Sweet Mango Lassi, this is a thinner, savory version. Just combine 4 cups (1 kg) of plain yogurt, 2 cucumbers (about 8 oz/250 g) peeled and diced, 1 cup (250 ml) of crushed ice, ½ teaspoon of salt, 1 teaspoon of toasted cumin seeds, and 2 tablespoons of chopped fresh mint in an electric blender and blend. Pour into four 8-oz (250-ml) glasses and serve.

VARIATION: MASALA SPICED LASSI—This spicy and refreshing drink is perfect for a hot summer day. Just combine 4 cups (1 kg) of plain yogurt, 6 tablespoons of chopped fresh coriander leaves (cilantro), about 20 fresh mint leaves, 1 small fresh green chili pepper, 1 teaspoon of salt, 1 teaspoon of toasted cumin seeds, and 1 cup (250 ml) of crushed ice in an electric blender and blend until smooth and frothy. Pour into four 8-oz (250-ml) glasses and serve.

VARIATION: AVOCADO LASSI—This variation is not traditional. This is my twist on the traditional lassi. Make sure it is consumed within a few hours of preparation or the avocado will turn dark. Just combine 2 cups (500 g) of plain yogurt, 2 large ripe avocado (about 1 lb/500 g) peeled and pitted, 4 teaspoons of sugar, 2 cups (500 ml) of water, 1 teaspoon of ground cardamom, and 1 cup (250 ml) of crushed ice in an electric blender and blend until smooth and frothy. Pour into four 8-oz (250-ml) glasses and serve.

Carrot Pudding with Nuts Gajar Halwa

I used to keep an eye out for a natural method to make this dessert as bright red here in the West as it is always made in India. Then, I discovered red, heirloom carrots! Use them to give this dessert a vibrant red hue. This dessert is a very popular dish for guests or a party. The pudding needs constant stirring while cooking for it to be gooey, fudgy, and absolutely delicious, but it's worth it. Serve with vanilla ice cream on the side for a special occasion.

Serves 6–8
Prep time: **15 minutes**
Cook time: **1 hour 50 minutes**

½ gallon (2 liters) whole milk
2 lbs (1 kg) carrots, peeled and grated
1 cup (200 g) granulated sugar
½ cup (100 g) ghee or unsalted butter
1 teaspoon ground cardamom, preferably
    freshly ground green cardamom seeds (from
    about 5 cardamom pods)
¼ cup (25 g) slivered almonds, toasted
¼ cup (30 g) golden raisins, soaked in warm
    water for 10 minutes, drained
2 tablespoons unsalted pistachios, chopped

Pour the milk into a large wide saucepan, bring to a boil and simmer, stirring often, until reduced to almost half; this will take about an hour.

Add the grated carrots to the reduced milk and return to a boil. Reduce the heat and simmer, stirring frequently, for about 30–40 minutes until all the milk has evaporated.

Add the sugar and simmer, stirring to dissolve. Continue to cook, stirring, until the carrots are quite dry. Add the ghee or butter and sauté well for 20–25 minutes. Stir in the cardamom powder, toasted almonds, and raisins and then remove from the heat.

To serve, spoon the pudding into individual serving cups. Top with chopped pistachios and serve warm.

Steamed Yogurt Pudding

This is an inspired version of a very popular Bengali sweet called *mishit doi* (sweetened yogurt). This steamed version, served in a ramekin, is even more attractive when topped with raspberries or other fruit of your choice.

Serves 4
Prep time: **10 minutes plus 6 hours to drain the yogurt**
Cook time: **30 minutes**

2 cups (500 g) plain yogurt
1 cup (350 g) condensed milk
2 tablespoons golden raisins
¼ cup (30 g) finely chopped pistachios
Raspberries, to serve

Line a strainer with a double layer of muslin cloth and place over a large bowl. Pour in the plain yogurt, cover with a plastic wrap, and allow the whey to drain off for at least 6 hours or overnight in the refrigerator.
Preheat the oven to 350ºF (175ºC).
Whisk together the yogurt, condensed milk, and raisins until smooth. Divide the mixture between four small ramekins or ovenproof serving bowls. Cover each ramekin tightly with foil to prevent water from getting in. Place the dishes in a baking dish and pour in enough water to come a quarter of the way up the sides of the ramekins. Carefully place in the oven and steam bake for 30–35 minutes.
Cool the desserts in their dishes and chill overnight. Serve in their dishes or turn out onto serving plates. Serve with the raspberries and sprinkle the nuts over the top.

Tender Coconut Cooler
Nariyal Pani Thandai

Coconut water has a slightly sweet, somewhat nutty taste. Surprisingly, it doesn't taste like coconut. It has a flavor of its own. Coconut water has long been the most popular beverage consumed in the tropics, where it is considered not only a refreshing drink but a health tonic. Coconut water is a superfood filled with minerals, vitamins, antioxidants, amino acids, enzymes, and growth promoters. It is low in fat and has only a fifth of the sugar found in most fresh fruit juices. In my hometown of Udupi, we had more than thirty coconut trees in my backyard. Back then, buying was never a question for me! Here in the West, this beverage is gaining popularity. Some bottled varieties are available in stores, and it is served fresh in Asian markets. The addition of honey and salt makes it a refreshing drink for a hot summer day.

Serves 4
Prep time: **10 minutes**

3 cups (750 ml) coconut water, chilled
½ cup (125 ml) freshly squeezed lemon juice
6 cups (1.5 liters), sparkling water or club soda, chilled
½ teaspoon salt
3 tablespoons honey
1 cup (150 g) chopped fresh tender coconut meat, to serve
Lemon slices, to serve

Blend together all ingredients except the fresh tender coconut flesh.
Pour into four, tall 8-oz (250-ml) glasses. Serve garnished with fresh tender coconut and lemon slices.

Tamarind Cooler Imli Paani

This is my take on a popular street drink that is known as *jal-jeera* or *jeera paani*. This tangy-spicy drink is served at roadside eateries around northern India. It is a much-loved summer beverage because tamarind is thought to have a cooling effect on the body. It's best served as a before-dinner drink with any salad or snacks. Tamarind is easily available in Asian, Mexican, and Indian markets.

Serves 2
Prep time: **10 minutes**

1 tablespoon tamarind paste
3 cups (750 ml) water, chilled
2 tablespoons freshly squeezed lemon or lime juice
3 cups (750 ml), sparkling water or club soda, chilled
¼ teaspoon salt
½ teaspoon ground cumin (optional)
1 tablespoon candied ginger chopped (optional)
1 tablespoon honey
3 tablespoons sugar
Crushed ice or ice cubes, to serve
Lemon slices, to serve

Place all the ingredients together in a shaker. Shake well, pour into highball glasses over ice, and serve garnished with lemon slices.

Tender Coconut Cooler

Tamarind Cooler

The Perfect Chai

We Indians love our chai! For some of us, it evokes memories of the gorgeous Indian monsoons, and for others, it's simply a stress-reliever enjoyed since youth. Today, not surprisingly, even your local Starbucks has chai crème latte on its regular menu. Here, I've provided the traditional recipe. Try it once and you are sure to be hooked! I can't get enough chai—it's my best family-time beverage and the perfect start to a busy workday.

Serves 2
Prep time: **5 minutes**
Cook time: **10 minutes**

2 cups (500 ml) water
¼ teaspoon fennel seeds
1 piece peeled fresh ginger, 1-in (2.5-cm) , lightly crushed
6 green cardamom pods, crushed
½ cup (125 ml) milk
2 teaspoons loose black tea leaves or 1 black tea bag, preferably English breakfast
Sugar, for serving

Bring the water, fennel seeds, ginger, and cardamom to a boil over high heat in a medium saucepan. Lower the heat to medium and continue to boil for another minute to extract maximum flavor.

Add the milk and bring to a boil once again. Add the tea leaves and remove from the heat. Cover the pan and set aside to steep for about 3 minutes.

Pour the mixture through a strainer into 2 teacups. Discard the spices. Serve hot with sugar on the side.

Shopping Guide

Indian markets can seem intimidating at first, but a trip to one is well worth it. The experience may encourage you to be adventurous and experiment with new ingredients. I always appreciate the range of fresh produce, spices and dry foods, such as rice and Indian lentils, available at such markets. These items also tend to be more affordably priced in an Indian market than at regular supermarkets. Here are a few of my favorite stores for Indian food and spices. Many of these stores also sell Indian clothes, specialized Indian cookware, and Indian music and Bollywood movies.

BHARAT BAZAAR
11510 West Washington Boulevard
Los Angeles, CA 90066
(310) 398-6766

BOMBAY SPICE HOUSE
1036 University Avenue
Berkeley, CA 94710
(510) 845-5200

BOMBAY BAZAAR
548 Valencia Street,
San Francisco, CA 94110
(415) 621-1717

COCONUT HILL INDIAN MARKET PLACE
554 South Murphy Avenue
Sunnyvale, CA 94086
(408) 738-8837

FOODS OF INDIA
121 Lexington Avenue #28
New York, NY 10016
(212) 683-4419

KALUSTYAN'S
123 Lexington Ave
New York, NY 10016
(212) 685-3451
www.kalustyans.com

PATEL BROTHERS
2610 W. Devon Avenue
Chicago,IL 60659
(773) 262-7777
www.patelbros.com
(The above location in Chicago is the flagship store, they have stores all over the US—see website for locations.)

ASIA IMPORTS, INC.
1840, Central Avenue North East
Minneapolis, MN 55418
(612) 788-4571

Some good online resources for Indian Ingredients are:

VANNS SPICES, LTD.
www.vannspices.com
In addition to the website, its spices are available at gourmet food stores throughout the country (check website for store locations).

PENZEYS SPICES
www.penzeys.com
In addition to the website, its spices are available at gourmet food stores throughout the country (check website for store locations).

MORTON AND BASSETT SPICES
www.mortonbassett.com

SHOP INDIAN
www.ishopindian.com

SPICE SAGE
www.myspicesage.com

ETHNIC GROCER
A great online resource for ethnic items delivered to your doorstep
www.theethnicgrocer.com

INDIAN BLEND
www.indianblend.com

To locate any Indian grocery store and a good resource for anything Indian, go to www.thokalath.com

Index

Acknowledgments

I am always overwhelmed and humbled by the encouragement and support I get from my family, friends, and colleagues. This book is dedicated to all those people, and it belongs to them as much as it does to me. I enjoyed the process of making *The Café Spice Cookbook* and I could not have finished it without the significant influence and inspiration of many people. I will always remain thankful for all their ideas, insight, and tips that made my journey complete.

Special hugs to my amma and pappa, who gave me the undying support and the freedom to follow my dreams; to my loving family, which supports and motivates me to realize my passion and love for cooking; and to my life partner and best friend, Sreemoyee Sarkar, for her confidence and support through all the intense moments of pressure in my life.

Special thanks to Sushil and Lata Malhotra as well as Sameer, Payal, and Sandhya Malhotra—my Café Spice family—for being my pillars of support and advisors; and to all the dedicated team members at Café Spice who work hard to make this brand the best of the best. More like a family than merely colleagues, they have always supported and welcomed me with a smile and made my every day special.

A big thank you to all the wonderful and talented people who helped put this cookbook together, including everyone at Tuttle Publishing: Jon Steever and June Chong, my editors, for their stellar advice and support; and Eric Oey, who has always guided my vision for publishing cookbooks. Thanks to Sow Yun and the diligent and creative team that whipped this book into shape.

Huge thanks to the talented photographer and my friend, Jack Turkel, who always makes my vision for the food and settings come alive in his photographs and makes the food look sumptuous. I'd also like to thank Sambrita Basu, a dear friend and a writer who has helped turn my thoughts into reality for the book.

There are many more people—friends and mentors—whom I would like to thank, but a list of all of them would far exceed the limited dimensions of this page. To them I offer big thanks for their continuous support and belief in me.

Published by Tuttle Publishing, an imprint of Periplus Editions (HK) Ltd.

www.tuttlepublishing.com

Library of Congress Cataloging-in-Publication Data

Nayak, Hari.
  The Cafe Spice cookbook : 84 quick and easy Indian recipes for everyday meals / Hari Nayak ;
    photography by Jack Turkel.
      pages cm
  Includes index.
  ISBN 978-0-8048-4430-7 (pbk.) -- ISBN 978-1-4629-1517-0 (ebook) 1. Cooking, Indic.
    2. Cafe Spice (Packaged food supplier) I. Title.
  TX724.5.I4N2935 2015
  641.5954--dc23
                        2014030053

ISBN: 978-0-8048-4430-7

Distributed by
North America, Latin America & Europe
Tuttle Publishing
364 Innovation Drive, North Clarendon, VT 05759-9436 U.S.A.
Tel: (802) 773-8930; Fax: (802) 773-6993
info@tuttlepublishing.com; www.tuttlepublishing.com

Japan
Tuttle Publishing
Yaekari Building, 3rd Floor, 5-4-12 Osaki, Shinagawa-ku, Tokyo 141 0032
Tel: (81) 3 5437-0171; Fax: (81) 3 5437-0755
sales@tuttle.co.jp; www.tuttle.co.jp

Asia Pacific
Berkeley Books Pte. Ltd.
61 Tai Seng Avenue #02-12, Singapore 534167
Tel: (65) 6280-1330; Fax: (65) 6280-6290
inquiries@periplus.com.sg; www.periplus.com

17 16 15 14
10 9 8 7 6 5 4 3 2 1

Printed in Malaysia   1412TW

The Tuttle Story
"Books to Span the East and West"

Many people are surprised to learn that the world's leading publisher of books on Asia had humble beginnings in the tiny American state of Vermont. The company's founder, Charles E. Tuttle, belonged to a New England family steeped in publishing.

Tuttle's father was a noted antiquarian book dealer in Rutland, Vermont. Young Charles honed his knowledge of the trade working in the family bookstore, and later in the rare books section of Columbia University Library. His passion for beautiful books—old and new—never wavered throughout his long career as a bookseller and publisher.

After graduating from Harvard, Tuttle enlisted in the military and in 1945 was sent to Tokyo to work on General Douglas MacArthur's staff. He was tasked with helping to revive the Japanese publishing industry, which had been utterly devastated by the war. When his tour of duty was completed, he left the military, married a talented and beautiful singer, Reiko Chiba, and in 1948 began several successful business ventures.

To his astonishment, Tuttle discovered that postwar Tokyo was actually a book-lover's paradise. He befriended dealers in the Kanda district and began supplying rare Japanese editions to American libraries. He also imported American books to sell to the thousands of GIs stationed in Japan. By 1949, Tuttle's business was thriving, and he opened Tokyo's very first English-language bookstore in the Takashimaya Department Store in Nihonbashi, to great success. Two years later, he began publishing books to fulfill the growing interest of foreigners in all things Asian.

Though a westerner, Tuttle was hugely instrumental in bringing a knowledge of Japan and Asia to a world hungry for information about the East. By the time of his death in 1993, he had published over 6,000 books on Asian culture, history and art—a legacy honored by Emperor Hirohito in 1983 with the "Order of the Sacred Treasure," the highest honor Japan can bestow upon a non-Japanese.

The Tuttle company today maintains an active backlist of some 1,500 titles, many of which have been continuously in print since the 1950s and 1960s—a great testament to Charles Tuttle's skill as a publisher. More than 60 years after its founding, Tuttle Publishing is more active today than at any time in its history, still inspired by Charles Tuttle's core mission—to publish fine books to span the East and West and provide a greater understanding of each.